Mobilizing Web Sites

DEVELOP AND DESIGN

Kristofer Layon

Peachpit
Press

Mobilizing Web Sites: Develop and Design
Kristofer Layon

Peachpit Press
1249 Eighth Street
Berkeley, CA 94710
510/524-2178
510/524-2221 (fax)
Find us on the Web at: www.peachpit.com
To report errors, please send a note to errata@peachpit.com
Peachpit Press is a division of Pearson Education

Project Editor: Michael J. Nolan
Development Editor: Jeff Riley/Box Twelve Communications
Production Editor: Myrna Vladic
Copyeditor: Deborah Burns
Technical Editors: Zachary Johnson and Mike Resman
Proofreader: Jan Seymour
Interior Design: Mimi Heft
Cover Designer: Aren Howell Straiger
Cover Production: Jaime Brenner
Compositor: David Van Ness
Indexer: Valerie Haynes-Perry

ISBN 13: 978-0-321-79381-2
ISBN 10:   0-321-79381-1

9 8 7 6 5 4 3 2 1

Printed and bound in the United States of America

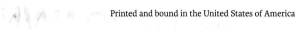

For Katie.

I've written two books,
but I still can't put into words
how much I love you.

ACKNOWLEDGMENTS

The goal of this book is twofold: to ease your entry into mobile design and development with examples and case studies, and to encourage and inspire you to start doing mobile work today, iteratively and in baby steps, by mobilizing web sites that you already work on.

So this book is not on the bleeding edge of mobile design approaches and techniques. Rather, it was inspired by many other designers, writers, and speakers who have informed my approaches to mobile design, content strategy, usability, and product management over the past several years. To document and pay homage to these sources of inspiration and best practices, I'm grateful that a number of them were willing to coordinate and contribute ideas and interviews about their work in mobile design and development: Ethan Marcotte, Colleen Jones, Luke Wroblewski, and the following people at Happy Cog—Rawle Anders, Stephen Caver, Greg Hoy, Mark Huot, Jenn Lukas, Yesenia Perez-Cruz, Greg Storey, Russ Unger, and Jeffrey Zeldman.

I'm also grateful for the contributions of Zachary Johnson, who was my main technical editor again after having that role for my first book. His corrections and suggestions for the HTML, CSS, and JavaScript examples in this book did much to improve and clarify my work. And I am grateful for the additional technical work of Mike Resman, my brilliant intern at the University of Minnesota who collaborated on the development of the first mobile web project I ever worked on. It's his technical skill that made that first project succeed, and it's also his work that made Chapter 10 of this book possible, as he was either the writer or editor of all of the PHP code that is featured there.

And thanks to Michael Nolan at Peachpit who had enough faith to have me write a second book. I think Michael and I were made for each other, as he feels that signing a project isn't necessarily about finding the right *expert* for a given topic. Rather, it's about finding the right *person*, at the right *time*, who has the right *idea*, and who can execute that idea *clearly* and *on time*. I will certainly agree that I am not a mobile expert, but I was excited to propose a book that sought to bring mobile design within reach of the everyday web designer and developer. I firmly believe that acceptable mobile design does not require an expert nor a ton of time and money—it just requires the decision to give it a try, and a commitment to keep improving on what you learn. That's what I am doing, and if this book inspires other people to get into mobile design and development, I will consider it to be a success.

Thanks also to my development editor Jeff Riley and the editorial and design staff at Peachpit, whose work led to this book looking as good as it does. And thanks to my supervisor at Capella Education Company, Jason Scherschligt, who was willing to hire me last spring as Capella's new Mobile Product Manager. I have the best mobile job imaginable and work with some of the brightest mobile designers and developers there are.

Finally and most importantly, I thank my family: Katie, Sarah, Grace, Emma, and Anne. You tolerated me leaving for work an hour earlier every day for several months to write this book. It wouldn't have happened without your support and encouragement.

CONTENTS

FOREWORD

Baby steps.

The phrase gets bandied about so much these days that we often lose sight of its significance.

A baby's first steps aren't just a few simple motions that get them started. They're a profound transformation from seeing the world move around us to taking part. Baby steps change our entire perspective and open up countless new opportunities to not only walk but run, skip, and dance. They're our entry into a whole new way of living.

The book in your hands (or on your screen) is also an entry into something new. Something so transformational it's fundamentally changing how we interact with our knowledge, our places, and with each other. That something is how we experience the Internet on mobile devices.

Always with us, always connected, fast and powerful mobile devices are taking over and redefining how we find answers, make purchases, share with others, and get things done. According to Jeremy Weinstein (http://goo.gl/Noq9L), in 2009, 50% of all new Internet connections worldwide came from mobiles. Gartner reports that by 2013, mobiles will overtake PCs as the most common web access devices worldwide (http://goo.gl/J64Zn).

If you've got an existing web site, chances are you're already noticing the transition and seeing your mobile traffic rising fast. But if do have an existing web site, do you need to start over to be relevant in the mobile age? How can you and your site adapt to such rapid change?

Baby steps.

Kris's book is filled with them—little but powerful things you can do today to adapt your current site to the changing web and the growing importance of mobile devices. These techniques will get you started without having to completely rebuild and redesign your current web site. But like real baby steps, they'll also open your eyes to new opportunities and ways of seeing the web. From there, who knows how far you'll go.

So what are you waiting for? Take those first steps now.

> —Luke Wroblewski
> Principal, LukeW Ideation + Design
> Author, *Mobile First* (A Book Apart)
> November 11, 2011

INTRODUCTION

FIGURE I.1 The IDS Tower in Minneapolis, the tallest office building downtown when it opened in 1974.

Whether it's "mobile first" or "mobile later," we are in the age of mobile computing and web browsing.

Don't let your web sites get left behind. Mobile later is better than not going mobile at all! More importantly, it can be your first step toward mastering mobile web design.

OVERCOMING THE FEAR OF "MOBILE NEVER"

Over the past few years, I have had the privilege of attending some great conference presentations about mobile app design and the mobile web. And if you have an interest in mobile and are reading this right now, you have also probably learned some valuable lessons and techniques to help you design new web sites for presentation on mobile devices.

The trouble for many of us, however, is that we often just go back to work and keep dreaming about designing that first mobile web site ... as we continue to work on our existing desktop-oriented projects. Many of us are in-house designers who help maintain and update several existing web sites, or maybe just one really large one. Or, we have contracts to continue maintaining and updating existing web sites for our clients.

But in these cases, we're not often in a position to propose an entirely new site design so that we can achieve our mobile goals.

So the rallying cry of "mobile first" might get us excited and inspired, but where does it leave those of us who are faced with "mobile later?"

Worse yet: what if we feel like our circumstances are keeping us locked into "mobile never?"

THIS IS NOT A UNIQUE PROBLEM

Among other factors, the allure of creating something new is what drives many of us into the field of web design. Images, text, and code: the thrill of filling an empty browser window with a new interactive design that we have created is exciting and satisfying. So when we are instead faced with incremental updates or improvements to existing web properties, it can feel more mundane. Where are the creative opportunities in that?

But sometimes we forget that working on the web is not any different from working with other media, materials, or mechanical systems. People get into a variety of creative fields because of the allure of starting from scratch and filling a blank canvas with something stunning and new—yet this is often the exception and not the rule. Take buildings as an example.

People who grow up wanting to design buildings often end up going to architecture school and, when they complete their programs, graduate as architects. Similarly, people who prefer a more hands-on experience of craftsmanship and construction attend a trade school to learn how to become a carpenter, mason, or other tradesperson. Regardless of the role, people who want to be engaged in the building design and construction fields are just as eager as web designers to make their mark on the world. They want to build something exciting that they can be proud of. And they usually dream about building something new (**Figure I.1**).

But for every big new construction project, there are many more renovation or improvement projects. These projects are what keep most architects and construction tradespeople busy most of the time.

I am fortunate to have worked in the architecture field prior to becoming a web designer, so this comparison is more than just metaphorical for me. As a graphic designer with a background in architectural history, I spent several years working for architects on a variety of tasks including historic building inventories and the design of client presentations. Despite my passion for new architecture (at that time, my plan was to get into architecture school after gaining some experience in the field while my wife was in graduate school), most of these firms' projects were renovations, additions, and reuse projects (**Figure I.2**).

But let's face it: often what is old becomes new again anyway, right? A renovation or reuse project isn't really just an old project with a new layer. It is a new project with a different set of constraints, and a unique set of existing conditions and context.

FIGURE I.2 The Mill City Museum in Minneapolis, which opened in 2003 as a museum, office, and apartment building. It was originally built in the 1870s as a flour milling complex.

MOBILE LATER

This is a cue to the world of web designers and developers: we, too, got into our field because we were excited to make something new. But as I noted earlier, this isn't always the case.

Or is it?

Re-contextualizing our work using the architecture example, we can see that a new web site does not always need to start from scratch. And in this particular case, a mobile web experience also does not need to start with a new web site. "Mobile later" can indeed work; we do not need to wait for "mobile first." And, actually, a great first step toward that elusive new "mobile first" site design is to start mastering the mobile web by taking baby steps and applying mobile techniques to an existing site design that you're already familiar with.

So how does this work, and where does one begin? That existing web site that you would like to mobilize for action in the 21st century of on-the-go web browsing seems rather hunkered down in a fixed-width, grid-based design that appears to be hopelessly mired in the 20th century.

If this is your fear, this book is written for you.

ABOUT THIS BOOK

As soon as you read that sentence, you may have thought, "It is? *Why* is this book for me? And why should I buy another book about mobile design? Hasn't this been written already?"

Yes and no. I have been collecting and reading a number of great books and articles about mobile design for the past few years, and they are all good in their respective ways. But they tend to fall into one of these categories:

1. Research-based analysis about the growth of mobile device use, and why now is the time for everyone to design for mobile devices. *Today.*

2. Higher-level, conceptual thinking about what makes a good mobile app or web site and how to plan such a project.

3. Visual examples of how to design screen layouts and user interfaces.

4. Technical, code-based techniques for developing web pages in a more responsive manner (usually focusing on CSS methods).

And when used as a library, these books and articles are all fabulous. In fact, I will refer to some of these writings in this book and its companion web site (www.mobilizingwebsites.net): they helped me get to where I am today, serve as a foundation for my ongoing work and writing, and are part of a shared base of knowledge for our evolving field.

But here are some things that distinguish this book:

1. As the title of the series implies, this book bridges the worlds of design and development. It gets you thinking about mobile design in a very holistic

manner, from the earliest stages of ideation and discovery at the very beginning of a mobile web project to usability evaluation at the end.

2. This book applies mobile planning, design, and coding techniques specifically to web sites that were initially designed for desktop display, which is what many of us deal with on a day-to-day basis. So all of the examples shown in the book including available code samples and pages to view at the book's companion site, http://www.mobilizingwebsites.net, are based on the common set of constraints of an existing fixed-width, grid-based web site.

3. The book organizes its suggestions and examples according to distinct mobile web challenges: how to present layouts, navigation, images, and text on small screen devices.

4. More importantly, this book helps you think about web mobilization *incrementally*. Mobilizing user experience, interface design, and content strategy does not need to be an all-or-nothing endeavor. Think about improving your web site like you would think about improving software or any product that is complex and long-lasting (and again, think about buildings). Smaller, incremental, but ongoing improvements can be just as challenging and rewarding to define and tackle as all of your improvements at once.

5. Finally, this book makes the case that after you become familiar with mobile constraints, techniques, and opportunities, and apply them to an existing site, you are then positioned to learn and do much more. Then you can have your site evaluated by users, rethink your content for mobile, and make the most informed decisions you can about making continued improvements. At that point, a more comprehensive "mobile first" redesign won't seem so daunting: it will feel like the right thing to do.

So if this is the book that mobilizes you into action today, and helps you apply mobile ideas and techniques that inspired you before you left them at the threshold of your office due to the common constraints of dealing with legacy web sites, I high-five you from afar.

Go forth and mobilize!

1

MOBILIZING USER EXPERIENCE DESIGN

To design well for mobile devices, it
is essential to begin with what is most
important: people. Because when you think about it, devices are
not really mobile by themselves. People are. And when people are
mobile, they often bring things with them.

Things that become mobile.

DEVICES AREN'T MOBILE: PEOPLE ARE

This book is actually about people. People are on the move: they get up in the morning and, if they are healthy, active, and either employed or busy with personal or family obligations, they probably are not going to spend all day in their homes. For many people, living is being mobile, underway, and on the go.

And given this, there are plenty of "mobile devices" that travel with people. We often are underway with devices of varied sizes including cars, bicycles, and watches. Some of these are high tech, and some of them not so much.

But if we are designing and developing for people, and for devices that connect to the web, we say that we are then designing for "mobile devices." But what this really means is that we are designing for the people who use these devices when they are on the move or not tethered to a desk. So how do we break this work down to some user experience (UX) design specifications that help us properly focus our thinking? Let's take a look and see.

MOBILE = **DOING**

Have you ever heard of the clever phrase "human *doing*" (as opposed to human *being*)? I will not dive into this too deeply or philosophically except to observe that people, most of the time, are usually not just *being* or existing. As I noted above, we are usually *doing* things. So as designers and developers, the best way to be tuned into how people will use what we are creating is to focus on what they will *do* with it. In user experience design, examples of what people will do with our product are called *user stories*.

As a designer and coder, I have to be honest with you: sometimes I just love getting into the technical details of design and development. And if you are like me, so do you.

But you know what? Our users—or customers—are probably not as technical as we are, at least not in the same ways that we are. And now that I work as a mobile product manager, it is my job to force myself (and the rest of my design team) to remember this every day, week in and week out. We might love to design and code, but in the end we are serving people and what they do. I'll cover how to organize and prioritize this vis-à-vis your designs later in this chapter.

FIGURE 1.1 The displays in a vehicle are a mobile interface, designed to be used on the go.

So what is important, in particular, about people doing things on the go? Let's take an example of driving your car, because this is something that most of us probably do and can relate to.

Even if you're driving around in a smaller town or city, driving is an activity that takes up most of your attention (at least, I hope it does!). Despite a lot of it becoming second nature over time, driving does quite a job of dominating both your senses and physical activity. You're pressing on the brake and accelerator, watching and listening for other cars or pedestrians, steering your vehicle, and paying attention to other information like the speedometer, fuel gauge, and so on. Plus, you might be listening to some music in the background, and possibly also the banter of your children or other passengers.

So what is my point?

Well, cars have been designed for mobile use for decades. And we can learn things from them.

The user experience of driving around and paying attention to surroundings means that the controls of vehicles (**Figure 1.1**) are designed for ease of use. They do not require an advanced degree to use. They are usually quite simple and intuitive. Lettering is clear and large, knobs are big, and graphics should be (though aren't always!) clear. Because when you're driving around town, you don't really want to be second-guessing what this indicator means or what that button does.

You need to know. Now. And it better be simple to identify and easy to read, grasp, push, pull, or otherwise implement.

So when designing a user experience for the mobile web, keep in mind how people are busy—and their senses are busy—when they are moving, driving, walking, or running. Immerse yourself in that experience and pay attention to how being busy shapes how you access information or take action. It will help you design a better user experience for the mobile web.

MOBILE = **DISTRACTED**

Beyond being busy, being mobile also means a certain amount of distraction.

Imagine being a parent who has brought his child to swimming lessons, and is then faced with taking a phone call on his mobile phone. And I, for one, do not really need to imagine this; this is me. I took part in a daily project stand-up meeting at work via Skype one day during my daughter's swimming lesson and this is what happened:

Not being a frequent user of Skype, I didn't realize that it does not switch as quickly between speaking and listening as regular cellular service does. In other words, when you speak on Skype, the other person is basically "muted" and you no longer hear what they're saying.

Well, the ambient sound of kids swimming in the pool, though not seeming like it was terribly loud, was enough to keep triggering the microphone on my iPhone and the sound kept cutting out as I was trying to listen to my colleagues talk in the meeting. So I left the pool's waiting area and went outside the swimming school, but that didn't help; there was even more noise out there. Increasingly distracted by my surroundings, I found myself feeling helpless: *WHAT DO I DO NOW?*

Fortunately, the good designers at Skype emulated the good designers at Apple and placed a rather large "Mute" button in the interface of Skype's mobile app. It's about an inch square: utterly enormous, quite a bit larger than it really needs to be for your finger.

FIGURE 1.2 A Skype call screen with Mute button activated. Note that this button is rather large. Large is good when it comes to buttons!

But it's not larger than it needs to be when you're frantically realizing that hitting the "Mute" button will solve your ambient noise problem as you try to listen to your colleagues back at the office (**Figure 1.2**).

Maybe it was good luck that this button is pretty darn big. Or maybe the designers anticipated that someone might be frantically looking for it in this kind of situation, and thus made sure that it wasn't just a garden-variety button of a more subtle stature. Regardless, learn from this example: when you're distracted (and possibly even frantic in your distraction), you need your options to be easy to spot. You need to be able to see your options in a millisecond.

Because if you're distracted, you have far less brain power to devote to finding what you need.

On the other hand, mobile usage is showing that not all "mobile" activity is happening on the go. But when it is not, there are other user mindsets to consider.

For example, some studies show that a lot of mobile usage is at home.

Why?

If you think about it, high mobile use at home should not be entirely surprising. Sure, laptops are convenient and quasi-mobile. They can quickly be set up on the kitchen table and, sometimes, people even properly respect their laptop's name and use them on their laps while sitting up in bed or in a comfy chair.

But the places and ways that tablets can be used at home are certainly more diverse. Lock the screen of an iPad and lie down sideways on your living room couch or sit out on the step in your front yard. And then think about smartphones: they go with us to bed, to the hammock or lawn chair, and—good heavens—sometimes even to the bathroom.*

If tablets and smartphones are going places that laptops are not, they are being used with different mindsets, too. I'm famous for taking out my iPhone on Sunday afternoons after brunch at my mother-in-law's house. Invariably, I'm tired and feel a nap coming on (and, more often than not, one does). So post-brunch, on the weekend, on a lazy Sunday, guess what kinds of user experiences I want to have? Nothing too taxing, thank you.

Such experiences should also be designed to be completed in a food-induced coma or in a decidedly unproductive mood. Simply put: I'm about as relaxed as I ever am during these moments, and I'm not about to put a lot of energy into my mobile device use. So if something is too much work, complex, or disruptive, I'll likely not use it in those situations—or, at the least, be annoyed when I do.

Consider this example from the Words With Friends mobile app. Words With Friends is a digital board game in which each player has a rack of seven letters, and you use them to create words on the board (much like another famous crossword-style board game that rhymes with babble). As you consider what words you can make when it's your turn, it's helpful to move the letters around on your rack to explore options.

------

*—So I hear.

FIGURE 1.3 A design update added the Shuffle button to improve the user experience.

A particularly cool detail in the digital adaptation of this word game is that it has an auto-shuffle feature for reordering your rack's letters. Earlier versions of Words With Friends took advantage of the device's accelerometer, requiring you to shake your device to shuffle the letters. This is pretty cool, but it's also a lot of work if you're trying to relax, disruptive if you're lying in bed next to your sleeping spouse, and nearly impossible if you're sitting next to someone on the bus.

So flash forward to the current release of Words With Friends which now features a new Shuffle button (**Figure 1.3**). The Shuffle button is really awesome if you don't like madly waving your phone around to shuffle your letters (though the company did not deprecate the shake-to-shuffle feature, for people who prefer a more kinetic experience).

Granted, until accelerometer support is more widespread via HTML5 and mobile browser support (at the time of this writing, it's supported by the mobile version of Safari on iOS devices), you will not be making user experience decisions about whether to employ device shake or a button for a mobile web function. But the point of this example is that context and user state of mind can and should have a profound influence on the UX solutions you consider when designing for mobile.

To support users in a relaxed state, do some work to understand the relaxed state of smartphone or tablet use. Yes, it's a bit of a paradox, but work really hard at getting into that relaxed mindset. And when you do, pay attention to how you hold mobile devices, navigate from screen to screen, and which details you find to be acceptable, annoying, troubling, or downright unacceptable.

MOBILE = **TASKS**

Another important mindset to consider is how mobile device and content use are often very task oriented. Whether people are on the go or using their mobile device at home, they are usually focused on completing a task.

People may be finding a recipe or making a shopping list, finding a location, looking up a date or time, checking a message, getting a price for something.

In fact, I find myself frequently defending these tasks with my children. To them, my iPhone seems to be all fun and games. So when they see me take my phone out at a time when they do not approve, they'll roll their eyes and say "Look, dad's playing on his phone AGAIN!" So I have to point out that, no, I'm not always *playing* on my phone (in fact, very little of my mobile use is for gaming); I'm probably getting an update on something or getting some small task done when I sense that I have a moment to do so.

And sure, I may be standing on the sidelines of a soccer field at one of my daughters' games. But if it's halftime and I want to get something done, what's the big deal?

On the other hand, halftime doesn't last long. I don't want to take any more time than is absolutely necessary to get the information I'm seeking. This means the user experience should be clear, concise, and minimize complex interactions or presentations. I don't want any additional noise in my mobile experience.

My children's critique of my frequent iPhone use is enough noise already, thank you very much!

TALK TO YOUR CUSTOMERS

So at the beginning of your mobile web discovery process, take a few steps away from your existing web site. In fact, just turn your computer off. You don't really need it at the beginning of user experience design, unless you're using it to type interview notes.

Because to mobilize your web site, you first need to mobilize your customers: mobilize them to help you. Set up some interviews, invite them to lunch or coffee, or just have some quick one-on-one meetings. Or if you have to, do this customer interaction over the phone or via email.

But go directly into the minds of your customers and find out what they really need to use your web site for if they are accessing it on the go. As the designer or business owner, you might think that one function or area of content is the most important, but you could be wrong. So remember who is always right: the customer, your web product's user.

And if you design for clients, be sure to get access to some of their customers. Understand the business and what customers need via mobile access. This is all about getting into their heads, and doing so all over again—even if you already did thorough user experience design for their first web site. In fact, you might be pleasantly surprised to learn how designing for mobile can help customers and clients focus on what is most important for their business relationship. But it's your responsibility to start this conversation and make sure that you take the time to do it thoroughly.

On a small screen, the constraints are much tighter. The customer's needs are in charge now, more than ever before.

WRITE USER STORIES

Even if you do not fancy yourself to be a user experience designer, don't get hung up on a job title. If you are not working with someone else who is in the UX designer role, you need to get into the practice of writing out user stories. They do not need to be complex, but they do need to exist. I have found them to be immensely useful as a designer and product manager.

User stories are really just abstract design specifications, but they are written in a narrative manner and focus on the user's actions and the context of those actions. Because after you talk to your customers, you want to capture what they need to accomplish with your mobile site in their terms. User stories are all about defining use cases. They are not about articulating design solutions.

Is that distinction clear?

Let's take an example. Here is what a user story is NOT:

"Frank is driving his family to the local water park. The car is loaded up and he wants to know the best route to get there before he starts driving. He takes out his smartphone, opens the water park's web site, selects the Directions tab in the upper right corner of the screen, then chooses the leftmost option labeled ..."

No, no, no. This user story starts off pretty well, but you can see that it immediately veers into the visual thinking that designers like to do. In short, it starts trying to define the solution within the definition of the problem.

Here is a better example of what a user story is:

"Frank is driving his family to the local water park. The car is loaded up and he wants to know the best route to get there before he starts driving. He takes out his smartphone, opens the water park's web site in the device's web browser, and looks for directions to the park."

Now this is a user story that you can sink your teeth into. Most importantly, it is a user story that will lead to a broader range of potential design solutions. Rather than pre-designing details of the solution, it leads to some additional questions for you to solve:

1. Do you need to break out an additional user story about how you would prompt a customer to bookmark this mobile web site on their home screen?

2. What needs to happen after the app opens in the browser? What will the customer want to do next?

User stories should be limited to the actions of users and the behaviors or reactions of the web site or application that they are using. By focusing on these activities at a high level and then getting more detailed—but initially always sticking to behaviors instead of features and design details—your initial mobile specifications will stay focused on customer needs and goals.

And this should ensure higher usability evaluations. So note that your user stories will eventually circle back to become tools for usability evaluation at the end of your project.

BREAK **USER STORIES** DOWN INTO **DESIGN REQUIREMENTS**

Once you have a set of concise user stories, you have the beginning of a story backlog that can guide your design and development work for your mobile web experience or application.

Let's revisit the need to get directions to the water park. How will Frank open the web site? It does not do this on its own. There are several ways of opening the web site, of course: typing in the URL, going to a bookmark in the browser, or the best option for a mobile web site that is used often is launching directly from your device's home screen.

With this tangible item, we just identified a few design requirements:

- Design a home screen icon

- Add appropriate support so that the user knows how to add your mobile web site to his home screen

As you continue looking through your mobile user stories, you can continue breaking the stories down into actionable requirements that involve tasks. Even at this point, you do not need to solve all of the design details: there is still plenty to do and explore. So keep the requirements and tasks at a high level; save the details for later.

CREATE A PRIORITIZED
STORY BACKLOG

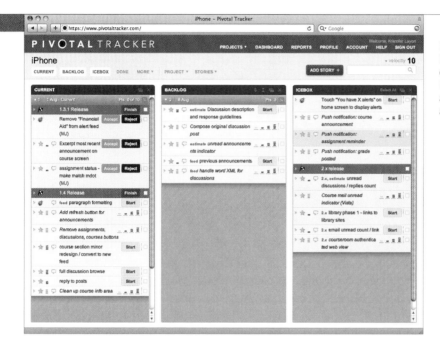

FIGURE 1.4 It's a good idea to keep your user stories in a project management tool. I use Pivotal Tracker, a fantastic web app that also has a companion app for iPhone and iPad.

A pile of user stories and requirements is itself not very helpful. To know where to begin, it needs a sequence. It requires priorities.

Prioritizing user stories is important because, as I noted earlier, mobilizing a web site does not need to be an all or nothing endeavor. You do not need to move directly from a site that is clunky and unusable on a mobile device to one that is an elegant and perfect example of mobile web design. There is plenty of room in between those extremes to offer an improved user experience.

Mobilizing a web site can and even should be an iterative process, just as iterative as any other aspect involving your web site. You allow your site architecture to evolve by adding a new section or pages from time to time, right? And I bet page content changes much more frequently. Apply the same thinking to your mobilization effort: it can change with time and does not have to assume that there is one "fully mobile" state to achieve prior to going live.

And as you track your user story backlog and its priorities, consider using a tool to help you manage this process (**Figure 1.4**).

FIGURE 1.5 The Kano Model helps us distinguish levels of customer satisfaction and fulfillment of needs across basic-, performance-, and excitement-oriented product features.

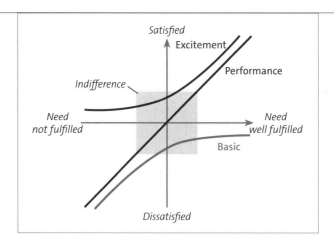

And as you try to prioritize your user stories, realize that this process does not need to feel as arbitrary as you might think it is. Priorities do not need to be cooked up merely according to your whims, even if there does not initially appear to be a clear reason why you might want to start with one story over another. To gain some clarity and have this be more systematic, it helps to apply some measures. I suggest using the Kano Model for prioritizing user stories.

THE KANO MODEL

The Kano Model (**Figure 1.5**) was developed by Noriaki Kano in the 1980s to help organizations tie product development to customer satisfaction. It helps deal with the seemingly fuzzy nature of prioritizing user stories by looking at different tiers of product attributes.

NOTE: For more information about the Kano Model, see http://en.wikipedia.org/wiki/Kano_model.

The tiers include:

- **Basic**: These are requirements that a product needs in order to perform well for a customer. There can still be degrees of necessity within this, but a requirement falls into this category because it is deemed quite essential—you would not want to release without these attributes. On the other hand, how well a basic requirement is delivered is easier to overlook, so it can also be more difficult to increase user satisfaction by improving a basic requirement.

  Taking an example of a car, some basic requirements would include an engine, wheels, and a steering wheel.

- **Performance**: These are requirements that a designed solution needs to differentiate itself from other similar solutions, based on how well it works and how happy this performance makes the user. Such requirements are in addition to basic requirements, and have the ability to drive higher customer satisfaction when designed and executed well. We tend to do a lot of our design work around improving performance requirements.

  In the example of the car, a performance requirement might be a GPS system, a turbo-charged engine, or leather seats.

- **Excitement**: The most challenging category of attributes is excitement. They are the opposite of basic: rather than being assumed and seen as an integral requirement of a product, an excitement attribute is not anticipated by the customer. And it is this special combination of surprise when they first use the feature, and elation if the feature is delivered well, that sends the user into orbit. So these attributes are quite rare and require a high level of creativity to tackle, but they can be the most valuable attributes to deliver when they are identified and then executed.

  Automobile features in this category could include Bluetooth connectivity with your mobile phone, or some other special feature that isn't really part of the standard driving experience—but makes spending time in that car extra special or convenient.

So the first step in prioritizing your user story backlog is deciding to what category each story belongs. As you do this, you also need to rank the categories according to the above user value. To keep it simple, each basic story would get 1 point, each performance story 2 points, and each excitement story 3 points. This is one level of sorting.

To add some additional discernment, you can also estimate the degree of change there will be for each user experience. Using a 5-point scale can assist you with this. For example, the current experience of finding a particular content area on your web site in a mobile browser might be terrible due to the size and placement of links on a page. So its initial ranking is 1.

If you decide on a fairly quick and easy way to improve this, but it's not your ideal solution that may take longer, you could rank the interim solution a 3. This recognizes an improvement in performance and value, yet also gives you room to grow if later you want to take improvement further.

The difference of 2 between the initial and improved state, multiplied by its category value (we'll say that this is a performance-level feature and assign it 2) yields a result of 4. This is your Kano improvement index. As you continue to estimate your features' categories and levels of improvement, you can see that this system can help parse your pile of user stories into a more meaningful list of priorities.

REFINE YOUR KANO INDEX PER YOUR AUDIENCE

One more tip regarding the Kano model: if you have different audiences or groups of customers and have a rough idea, based on analytics or other feedback, which group is more important to your business decisions and how they differ in their visiting patterns to your site, you can factor this into the Kano improvement index, too.

For example, if you have two features with overall values of 4 but one affects 75% of your site's visitors and the other feature only impacts 50% of your site's visitors, multiplying the 4s by .75 and .5 gives you an updated index of 3 for one feature and 2 for the other. This provides you with an additional level of sorting as you move through your prioritization process.

If you're savvy with spreadsheet software, you can set up your user story analysis with this software and have the spreadsheet software do these calculations for you.

WRAPPING **UP**

Because accessing the web on a mobile device is different than on a desktop or laptop environment and can vary so much between people and the contexts in which they are online, mobilizing web sites is a process that heightens the need for a thorough and disciplined approach to user experience. Mobile design is, quite literally, where I embraced UX design for the first time. And because I find UX to be so useful, I dedicated an entire chapter to it.

I hope that the tips and techniques I have outlined will help you get to know your customers better than ever and tie your mobile design priorities to their most critical needs.

Most importantly, I hope your UX analysis and results help you see how the rest of this book can assist you in the ways that make the most sense for your project. Because the rest of the book isolates web sites element by element, this will allow you to start designing mobile elements and experiences according to your own project's priority. But the order of these chapters does not imply the order in which you take them on (in fact, as you try focusing on your first mobile web site element by element, you'll realize that you'll actually need to focus on several things at once).

2

MOBILIZING **LAYOUT**

Changing the layout of a screen—that sounds a lot like redesigning a screen.

How can mobilizing a web site's layout be done without starting over with a new design?

STANDARDS-BASED LAYOUTS
ARE ALREADY RESPONSIVE

One of the first things to realize about mobilizing a web site is that you need to relinquish some control over positioning of elements. Not complete control, of course, just some.

But think about this for a moment: as Ethan Marcotte has articulated recently in his teachings about responsive web design, and others before him have been explaining for years—going back to the most ancient web scriptures of Jeffrey Zeldman—being a standards-based web designer is *inherently* about being responsive.

Think about the metaphor of surfing the web in this regard—it is *totally* appropriate, and not just from a user perspective but also from a designer perspective. We need to ride the waves, and carefully pay attention to conditions and context so that we can adjust our balance and course along the way. We cannot control the waves … but we can certainly adapt to them.

So if you are mobilizing a web site that uses CSS for layout, positioning, and styling, and HTML for content markup, you have already set the stage for a layout that can adapt to mobile devices and contexts.

And perhaps surprisingly, you have done this even if you used a fixed-width CSS layout. That's right, even a fixed-width layout isn't really fixed in the sense that it cannot change or be responsive. It's merely fixed for a certain set of conditions. So next we will prove this by using a fixed-width web site as our example for mobilizing a layout, as I would guess that most of us work with fixed-width layout web sites.

NOTE: To learn more about Ethan Marcotte's teachings on responsive design, see his book *Responsive Web Design* (A Book Apart). And to discover where the foundations of responsive design were first built, be sure to read Jeffrey Zeldman's *Designing with Web Standards* (New Riders).

WHAT MAKES IT **FIXED-WIDTH?**

To begin, let's start with what makes a fixed-width CSS layout appear to be "fixed" in the first place. The example used in this book is a common and well-established open source CSS framework called Blueprint, but what you will learn here should apply to any fixed-width layout that is governed by CSS. They all do the same thing, just varying in the details.

A fixed-width CSS framework does its work by doing two things:

1. It defines a systematic way of organizing the two-dimensional space of the screen, which is a fancy way of saying that it specifies units and measures for a grid.

2. It defines a nomenclature, or system of names, that can be used as CSS classes and IDs for consistently and (as much as the web allows) predictably presenting a web site's content within its grid-based layout system. These are the class and ID names that are then referenced in the HTML markup, on the content side of the house.

NOTE: For more information about Blueprint, visit www.blueprintcss.org.

UN-FIXING THE WIDTH

So if a fixed-width layout relies on those two elements marching in lockstep, the definition of units and measures on one hand and the referencing of CSS class names on the other, changing either one of them disengages the system. For example, if you specify this in your CSS:

```
.columnone {width: 400px;}
```

and you change a reference in your HTML from this:

```
<div class="columnone">...</div>
```

to this:

```
<div class="columntwo">...</div>
```

then the 400px width that is defined for the columnone class in the CSS will no longer be applied to the content contained within that <div>. So changing a class name in the HTML by itself does not help you change the layout of your page or screen unless you have another class that is ready to help you out with the new units, measure, position, or some combination of these.

Plus, changing the classes in your HTML would obviously be a major pain! And that's clearly not the intention of web standards; the intention is quite the opposite. If you have built a system of class names that can be redefined on the CSS side of the house, you're ready to make changes there instead. In just one place ... but in a way that can change the behavior of those classes across an entire web site, no matter how many pages there are.

So what you will be doing instead looks more like the following: You will start with something like this in your CSS:

```
.columnone {width: 400px;}
```

and instead change the specification of what columnone does for the layout by redefining it in your CSS:

```
.columnone {width: 600px;}
```

By taking this approach, you can specify new units and measures for the existing HTML elements in your web site that you want to optimize for mobile presentation.

Ready to start putting this concept into action?

SHUFFLING THE SQUARES

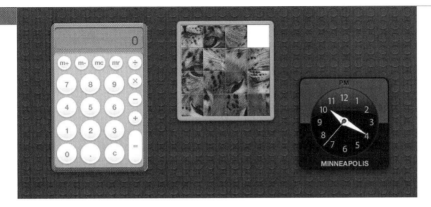

FIGURE 2.1 The sliding tile puzzle in the Mac OS X dashboard (middle).

Remember the sliding tile puzzles where you have to reconfigure the grid of image fragments into a complete image? You solve the puzzle by sliding the images around, one at a time, into the opening that is left in the grid. Beginner puzzles have 8 tiles in a 3 by 3 grid; puzzles that have 15 tiles in a 4 by 4 grid are quite a bit more challenging.

If you haven't played one of these for a while, take a break and see if your computer has a digital version. Macs do in their dashboard widgets (**Figure 2.1**)!

The layout behavior of web browsers is very similar to the behavior of these tile puzzle games. Even a very simple page of text reconfigures itself when you drag the corner of a browser window around to resize it. As the width changes, the lines of text adjust themselves to move and fill the "empty space" that is being created at the bottom of the window. Or, from the other perspective, the narrowing window is squeezing the text lines into shorter ones. Well, really, both of these things are happening at the same time (**Figure 2.2** and **Figure 2.3** on the next page).

FIGURES 2.2 and **2.3**
Resizing a browser window demonstrates how browsers and web sites are already designed to be responsive. The content adjusts to fill the space of the viewport. The first image is 1024×768 pixels and the second has been resized to 768×735.

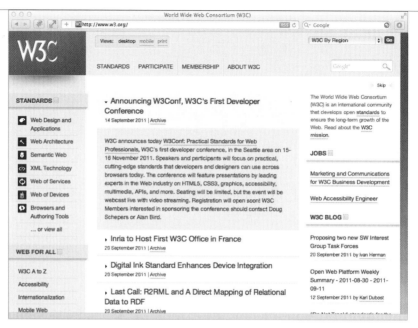

The point is this: the viewports of browser windows are inherently responsive. They are designed to be more elastic versions of the ancient sliding tile puzzle games. And instead of the pieces being uniform squares, the parts—words, paragraphs, images, blocks, divs—all adjust as space is created or taken away, pushed, or stretched.

A fixed-grid CSS layout can be made to behave the same way, such that this can be the basic principle behind mobilizing such a layout from a larger-format desktop presentation to a small-screen mobile presentation. In fact, a fixed-grid is also usually inherently responsive within the responsive browser viewport. So how do we take advantage of these properties for mobile presentation and also rein them in a bit as needed to promote as much consistency as possible in our mobilized outcomes?

The rest of this book will show you how to mobilize web content *without rewriting all of your HTML markup*. That's right: if you already have a web site with a CSS layout, you should be able to learn how to mobile-optimize your web site today, without any substantial redesign or recode. You will be able to do this because of the inherent responsiveness of browsers that we've just reviewed.

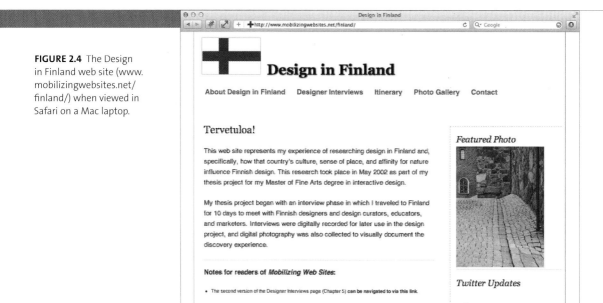

FIGURE 2.4 The Design in Finland web site (www. mobilizingwebsites.net/ finland/) when viewed in Safari on a Mac laptop.

With some solid web standards theory and browser mechanics in mind, now it's time to turn our attention to a web site that we can mobilize. I have designed a small web site (**Figure 2.4**) to update for presentation on mobile devices. It is typical in many respects, so I hope this makes it familiar to you, even if you are not particularly interested in or familiar with design in Finland (though I happen to be; half of my ancestors are from Finland, and one of my best friends also lives there).

Note some of the aspects of the site:

- **Fixed width**: Like many web sites, it has a fixed-width design (950 pixels, using the Blueprint CSS framework). This is fairly common for existing web sites, as it should be. Some designers advocate for fluid layouts, but fluid layouts can be really problematic because readability decreases when line lengths exceed 66 characters. Therefore, a fluid layout on a wide screen is a bad design (unless the text size scales up with the width).

FIGURE 2.5 The Design in Finland web site (www.mobilizingwebsites.net/finland/) when viewed in Mobile Safari on an iPhone.

- **Horizontal navigation**: Horizontal navs are quite typical. More importantly, the lessons you'll learn here will apply to existing navigations whether they are horizontal or not.

- **Multi-column layout**: This site has a page template with a primary content area and a narrower right column to highlight related content.

- **Header and footer**: Again, quite common in most web page designs.

So what does this look like on a mobile handset like an iPhone? See **Figure 2.5**. Pretty small indeed. So let's mobilize this site, shall we?

> **NOTE:** Please note that the original non-mobilized version of this web site is online at http://www.mobilizingwebsites.net/nonmobilized/. If you want to follow along, download this site at http://www.mobilizingwebsites.net/nonmobilized/download.zip (2.7MB) and make your changes to those files as described in the rest of the book.

MOBILE HTML

As we begin, a small caveat: it's not possible to do this without *any* rewriting of your HTML. You have two small changes to make to the top of your HTML pages and, because these are in the head of the page, they should be one-time changes in your site's page template.

TIP: Uh, you did template your site when you built it, right? If you didn't, a find-and-replace across all of your site's pages will accomplish the same thing.

The first tiny change involves exerting some additional control on your user's browsers by instructing these browsers to make the width of the viewport (that is, the area within the frame or "chrome" of a browser window that displays content) the same as the width of the device screen and to make this a 1:1 relationship for the units and measures that are specified in a new mobile CSS file:

```
<meta name="viewport" content="width=device-width,
  initial-scale=1.0" />
```

Note that this will not impact how a regular desktop or laptop browser will present your web site (unless you narrow the browser window below the max-width that we define in the mobile stylesheet).

Second, you need to link to a new mobile stylesheet:

```
<link href="css/blueprint/screen.css" rel="stylesheet"
    type="text/css" media="screen" />
<link href="css/blueprint/print.css" rel="stylesheet"
    type="text/css" media="print" />
<link href="css/main.css" rel="stylesheet"
    type="text/css" media="screen" />
<link href="css/mobile.css" rel="stylesheet" media="screen
    and (max-width: 768px)" type="text/css" />
```

Note that the mobile stylesheet is added after the standard CSS framework stylesheets and the site's `main.css` stylesheet.

So what does this second tiny edit of your HTML do? It incorporates a *media query*, and instructs the web page that if the screen width is under 768 pixels in width, it will use the rules in `mobile.css` to determine the positioning, units, and measures of your page. In doing so, any styles that are redefined in this stylesheet will trump the styles already defined in the previous stylesheets.

WHY **768 PIXELS**?

For the examples in this book, I'm using 768 pixels because it is the narrowest dimension of the iPad and iPad 2 screen. This max-width (with the meta tag setting) was tested on iPhone, iPhone 4, and the two standard sizes of Android handheld devices. This max-width was also tested on iPad; the site renders as full-screen in landscape mode, and uses the mobile styles in portrait mode. For additional tweaking of how you might set media queries for additional conditions on tablets or other devices, see Ethan Marcotte's chapter about media queries in his book *Responsive Web Design* (2010: A Book Apart).

FIGURE 2.6 (left) The Design in Finland web site (www. mobilizingwebsites.net/ finland/) when viewed in Mobile Safari on an iPhone after changing the viewport width to the device width.

FIGURE 2.7 (right) The Design and Finland web site after the width has been redefined.

MOBILE CSS

Now that you link to a new mobile stylesheet, you need to evaluate which styles to modify to make the layout work better for mobile presentation.

After changing the viewport and attaching a blank mobile.css stylesheet, **Figure 2.6** shows what you get for a result on a mobile device.

So what is the main problem here? What is happening is that the page is behaving exactly as instructed: it is adjusting the viewport to show the same amount of pixels (320) as the iPhone's viewport size. The trouble with this is that you have not yet redefined any of the widths of the Blueprint-defined divs in the layout—it is still treating the page as 950 pixels wide. Which means we are only seeing about a third of the page as the rest runs off the screen.

So let's look at the divs that wrap all of the content. There are several:

- **Class names**: container, span-24, span-15, span-7

- **ID names**: banner, nav, bodycontent, rightbar, footer

I bet if you rescale all of these classes and IDs to be width=100%, that should solve everything, right? So let's hit them all with that specification, just to be safe— and also set the margin and padding to zero while you're at it:

```
.container, .span-24, .span-15, .span-7 {
    width: 100%;
    margin: 0;
```

```
    padding: 0;
}


#banner, #nav, #bodycontent, #rightbar, #footer {
    width: 100%;
    margin: 0;
    padding: 0;
}
```

Let's take a look now (**Figure 2.7**).

Well, you're not quite done mobilizing this site yet—not by a long shot. But you can certainly see how this is starting to work because now the content is being constrained to the width of the screen.

But as I scroll down the screen, I see that I forgot to remove the borders that I have in the desktop version of this web site, borders that help define the edges of the divs and help provide some visual structure and style to this page layout. They do not serve any purpose in this new mobile layout (other than make it look bad), so they need to be removed:

```
.container, .span-24, .span-15, .span-7 {
    width: 100%;
    margin: 0;
    padding: 0;
    border: none;
}


#banner, #nav, #bodycontent, #rightbar, #footer {
    width: 100%;
    margin: 0;
    padding: 0;
    border: none;
}
```

FIGURE 2.8 The Design in Finland web site (www.mobilizingwebsites.net/finland/) when viewed in Mobile Safari on an iPhone after redefining the divs to be device-width and without the unnecessary borders.

Also, there's one more thing that you need to tweak before checking. Because the #bodycontent div is specified with the Blueprint class `.span-15 append-1`, you need to take the append-1 portion into account in the width. In other words, setting `.span-15` to width=100% doesn't work because the append-1 still adds some space to the width. And you also can't set the compound `div.span-15 append-1` to width=100%, either (I tried, and it doesn't work). So you need to address the ID (bodycontent) with a new specification instead, setting it to something narrower than 100%—I figured out that 90% does the trick.

Finally, I'm also adding some margin as long as I'm at it. So here's the additional CSS rule that targets the bodycontent ID:

```
#bodycontent {
    width: 90%;
    margin: 20px;
}
```

So now let's take a look at the fruits of our labor (**Figure 2.8**).

Not bad! This is looking like a decent start for a mobile layout. It doesn't need to be much more difficult than this. Granted, it can take a little experimentation to figure out some of the more quirky CSS adjustments (like the bodycontent ID in this example—that took a while to troubleshoot). But any design exercise requires some experimentation, so don't be too timid about that. Dive in to your own code and apply what you've learned here.

> **NOTE:** There is another layout issue to consider when mobilizing existing web content: deciding whether you want to hide any content. So we'll touch on some aspects of that issue next (and other aspects of it later in Chapter 5).

TO DISPLAY OR NOT TO DISPLAY?

A hot topic in mobile design (as in, it gets some people really hot under the collar!) is when designers choose to not display a div or two of content if it is deemed secondary and not important enough to present in a mobile web site.

The argument against this is pretty simple and easy to appreciate: when browsers are told to not display some content via CSS:

```
#supplemental {display: none;}
```

you need to realize that the browser is doing exactly that—not displaying the content. But the CSS did not (and can not) tell the HTML not to *load* the content. So the content is still downloaded to the mobile device, often over a cellular network, and therefore is often using up a few bytes of someone's data plan.

Now I can appreciate this and, at face value, it can initially make it seem silly or even wrong to ask a mobile browser to download an extra div of content that is not going to be displayed.

Except that the content was going to be downloaded anyway, so what's the difference?

The gap in the logic is that the mobile browser is downloading *extra* content. Well, it's extra in the sense that it won't be displayed—but it's the *same* content that would have been downloaded anyway had the display of it not been set to none.

So short of redesigning a web site using a mobile first approach (which is a great idea if you have the time and budget to do so) and doing a complete content inventory and rewrite, mobilizing an existing web site seeks the most mobile-optimized results you can with the HTML that you already have.

And this is where I think the logic of using `display:none` starts to make sense again, because I think we can argue that having a mobile-optimized site—even if the HTML itself has not been redesigned and optimized—still offers significant value. Enough value, arguably, that someone downloading the unseen content shouldn't necessarily mind paying a penny or two more for the privilege of seeing the site optimized for their small screen. The same penny or two that they would have paid, incidentally, to see more than they should (and at a size so small that it requires significant pinching and zooming, which comes at its own cost).

Plus, consider the value of this from the business owner's perspective. If a tiny mobile tax of a few pennies means a more mobile-optimized web experience that could make the difference between a sale/conversion or not, doesn't everyone win in this scenario?

So, this is my argument. You do not have to agree, but you should at least consider the extremely low cost of requiring someone to download a little content that won't be displayed. After all, you probably do not think twice about the bandwidth used when people download all of your extra SEO meta data in your page header, do you? (Because they don't see that either!)

In the end, and for the example in this book, I am opting to not display the `rightbar` div on each page. It is 13 lines of code and not quite 400 characters, which is a pretty small amount of code to download but not display. Yet to display it makes the mobile version of the page nearly twice as long. And while I think the sidebar works well for the desktop version of the site, I don't think it's important enough to include in the mobile version.

WRAPPING **UP**

After making only two minor changes to the HTML in the head of your page template, you can open yourself up to the world of mobilizing an existing web site without having to start over from scratch with an entirely new mobile first design (which could still be the perfect solution for you in your longer term web strategy). But if you don't have the time or budget to do that now, mobilizing what you have now is the next best thing.

Because you can do it now. *Today*.

After attaching a mobile stylesheet as HTML edit number two, this chapter helped you understand how to optimize a fixed-width page layout for mobile presentation. It's not too hard, really, and you already did a bunch of the work months or years ago when you first designed the site—if you used web standards. Because your site was already designed to be responsive; with new mobile styles, you're merely teaching your web site to be even more responsive.

And as part of this responsiveness, you now better understand the cost of choosing not to display some content that your users will still download. If it's a small amount of content, it's not a significant cost to your users ... especially if they appreciate the new mobile results that you will be delivering. So weigh your options carefully, and decide what is best for your audience, project, budget, and schedule.

PROJECT INTERVIEW 1

ARIZONA STATE UNIVERSITY AND THE MTV O MUSIC AWARDS

It's interesting to hear about how a "mobile later" approach can compare to a "mobile first" approach. Because such decisions aren't just limited to certain categories of designers or clients—they can impact anyone, and can even arise mid-project.

FIGURE PI 1.1 The Arizona State University Online web site in a desktop browser.

Such was the case for Happy Cog, an agency with offices in New York, Philadelphia, and San Francisco. Thanks to the eight people who contributed to these two interviews, and also to Happy Cog's founder Jeffrey Zeldman, who connected me to these projects and their staff:

Rawle Anders, Client Services Director

Stephen Caver, Designer/Developer

Greg Hoy, President

Mark Huot, Technology & Development Director

Jenn Lukas, Interactive Development Director

Yesenia Perez-Cruz, Designer

Greg Storey, President

Russ Unger, User Experience Director

FIGURE PI 1.2 The Arizona State University Online web site in a mobile browser.

HOW DID YOU MANAGE THE ARIZONA STATE UNIVERSITY PROJECT?

We worked with ASU Online, the department responsible for facilitating online courses. At the beginning of the project we asked the client to identify their project manager who would become our sole contact throughout the project. During large project milestones—which include reviews of our user experience, design, and template deliverables—we would meet with the larger group, who had a shared responsibility for the work we produced.

DID YOU HAVE TO HELP CONSTRAIN THE PROJECT SO THAT IT WASN'T TOO DIFFICULT TO ACCOMPLISH, OR DID ASU HAVE A REASONABLE GOAL FOR MOBILE ALREADY?

ASU recognized the need for mobile and had other projects underway including an iPhone application used for social networking with other "online" students. And for this project, a mobile strategy was included as part of the scope of work, but only if there were adequate resources available after completing the primary task of redesigning the web site.

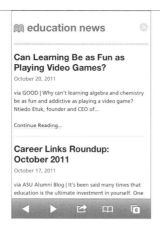

FIGURE PI 1.3 The Arizona State University Online web site in a mobile browser.

DID HAPPY COG PROVIDE MOBILE UX DESIGN, DEVELOPING THE SITE, AND MOBILE USABILITY EVALUATION?

No, the decision to address mobile was not decided upon until later in the project (via a change request), and the lengths to which we addressed this need were largely based on estimated hours remaining at that point. So due to this late decision, many of the elements of the responsive design process—content prioritization exercises and the creation of wireframes for responsive states—were not done until after UX and design phases were completed.

SO SIMILAR TO THE EXAMPLES IN THIS BOOK, RESPONSIVE MOBILE DESIGN WAS ADDED TO AN EXISTING SITE DESIGN. IN THAT CASE, WHAT WERE THE CLIENT'S EXPECTATIONS FOR YOUR MOBILE RESULTS?

Stephen Caver built responsive templates with flexible grids and media queries based on his assessment of how to best render the templates for varying screen dimensions. So we did not design the site with responsive states accounted for along the way. We suggested this as an option to ASU Online and their team to address their concerns about the need for a mobile strategy, and make the new site accessible for contexts other than a standard web browser. After we got into the project and realized that we wouldn't have enough hours for a separate mobile site, we settled on responsive design as the best approach.

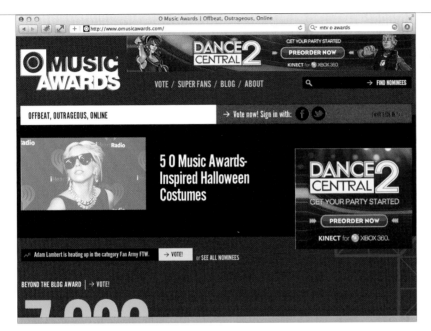

FIGURE PI 1.4 The MTV
O Music Awards web site
in a desktop browser.

UNLIKE THE ASU ONLINE SITE, O MUSIC AWARDS APPEARS TO
BE A TIGHTLY-FOCUSED MOBILE SITE—ALMOST AN APP—THAT
IS DESIGNED MORE FOR A LIMITED TASK. HOW MUCH OF THE
VOTING FOR O MUSIC AWARDS IS DONE VIA MOBILE?

Unfortunately, we don't have specific numbers just yet. However, what we can tell
you is that only 8% of the traffic is coming from a mobile device. On the desktop,
the site's most popular pages are the popular category pages that facilitate voting.
On mobile, the most popular pages are much more varied, suggesting that users are
browsing more than voting while mobile. What's interesting is that we're seeing a
good percentage of mobile visits out of the US, where typically we've experienced
fewer mobile visitors (USA: 15% mobile, London: 11% mobile, Japan: 25% mobile).

FIGURE PI 1.5 The MTV O Music Awards web site in a mobile browser.

DID MTV HIRE YOU TO DO MOBILE, OR DID YOU BRING MOBILE TO THE PROJECT?

MTV, as a company, has always been a proponent of mobile design. Before responsive, they supported feature phones back to some of the earliest Video Music Awards shows. The O Music Awards are no different. MTV came to Happy Cog knowing they needed to support a mobile generation. Happy Cog was able to work with MTV to provide a responsive approach that blended traditional mobile design (mobile specific ads, device tailored video experiences) with all the benefits of a responsive design (single code base, unified user experience). This is MTV's very first responsive site. It works within their existing advertising rules without losing all the benefits of responsive design.

HOW DID YOU ARRIVE AT RESPONSIVE DESIGN BEING THE RIGHT APPROACH?

It's actually not just responsive—it's also a mix of adaptive and fluid. We got together to discuss the approach we wanted to take for displaying the design on different screen sizes. While a completely responsive approach, including fluid grids and fluid images, is a great solution for some sites, we didn't think it was the best answer for this specific design. We decided to keep the optimal layout intact until users reached a width below 768 pixels, and then began to optimize the layout using media queries. At that point, we started to swap static columns for fluid

FIGURE PI 1.6 The MTV
O Music Awards web site
in a mobile browser.

ones. We then fine-tuned the CSS for specific mobile device targets to make sure
smart phones received a catered composition. We wanted the changes in the aesthetic to be the least distracting as possible, while keeping the focus on the voting
functionality and content. We found this approach worked best for this project.

WHAT WAS THE PRIMARY GOAL OF THE
O MUSIC AWARDS MOBILE SITE?

The main goal of this mobile site was to promote voting and sharing. When designing the small screen versions, it was important to make sure that the voting process
was as clear and easy as possible. On smaller screens, we hid elements that were
ancillary and not crucial to the experience. Because of the tight timeline, there were
no Photoshop comps created for small screens. Instead, design and development
worked together looking at the design in the browser and adjusting text sizes and
layout as needed.

IN WHAT PHASES OF THE MTV O AWARDS
SITE WAS HAPPY COG INVOLVED?

Happy Cog played a role throughout the development of this project's mobile design.
The Happy Cog team played a pivotal role, from consulting with their mobile team
to meet specific advertising regulations, to working through front-end UX design.

3

MOBILIZING
NAVIGATION

Mobile devices aren't new—we've already had them for decades, even centuries. Let's take a look at a few of them, and also look at some mobile apps, to help understand how to better design a web site's navigation for mobile use.

As I noted in Chapter 1, the era of iOS, Android, and other mobile operating systems and their related hardware have us talking a lot about "mobile devices." These phones, smartphones, handhelds, MP3 players, tablets—they're revolutionary in many ways, to be sure.

But they're not the only mobile devices that we have. So let's take a look at some interfaces from other mobile devices to see how they are designed. Are there some lessons that we can learn and then apply to mobile web design?

WATCHES

FIGURE 3.1 A dashing pocket watch.

Years ago, it was common for a guy to have a pocket watch. These watches were serious timepieces, and had beautifully-rendered analog displays.

What do you see when we look at the watch shown in **Figure 3.1**?

First, a classic watch like this one is clearly a mobile device. It's not digital technology, but it was certainly designed to hang from a fancy vest pocket and go wherever we went. It's designed to be mobile. Some of the ways that it has been optimized for mobility:

SIZE

Granted, you can get some rather large watches (in fact, some pocket watches were rather gargantuan!). But this watch, as many are, is fairly small and scaled nicely to the hand. It is thin, light, and meant to be worn without much trouble or distraction.

Well, maybe not without *any* distraction; they were also designed to be noticed!

SCALE

The face (or "screen") of the watch and the information on it are scaled to a variety of factors. Note the proportion of watch face to the rest of the watch body; it is very large. Rather similar to a smartphone or tablet screen, really. Today we marvel at the impressive designs we are seeing on nicely designed handheld devices like the iPhone 4 or (at the time of this writing) the newest Samsung Android tablets. Compared to laptops, they certainly are elegant; compared to a nice watch, they're actually not so revolutionary. They're just being designed as well as some of our other well-designed mobile devices.

DESIGN

The data elements of a watch face are also scaled and designed for mobile use. A variety of techniques help to accomplish this. A nice watch face has hands and numbers that are easy to read at a glance, so size and typography are factors. And part of the legibility or readability of these elements is color and contrast.

CAR INTERFACES

FIGURE 3.2 A dashing dashboard display.

Sometimes when I'm thinking about the design of mobile web interfaces, I marvel at how much they make me think of car interfaces. We typically do not think of car displays and buttons as interfaces, but they most definitely are. Whether they are digital and computer-like or analog and more tactile, they are the connections between the people and a vehicle's data, and provide us with the ability to navigate the vehicle from place to place (**Figure 3.2**).

Huh, *navigate*. Interesting how that word is used on the web, isn't it? Indeed, cars should definitely be a brief focus of our study if we are gearing up to design for mobile web browsing!

SIZE

In cars, size matters—just as it does for watches. But here the lessons are somewhat different. What is useful here is to see that in cars, there is usually a lot of consideration about the size of controls. Whereas a watch is too small to have buttons that are properly scaled to the human finger, a car has plenty of space to accommodate larger buttons that scale well to our fingers.

POSITION

Another good lesson we can learn from cars is positioning. The size of controls is one matter; where they are located is quite another. Distance from the driver, proximity to other controls, and how various controls are grouped are all incredibly important factors in a vehicle user's experience. Some car manufacturers are, in fact, known for or specifically market their advantage in the design of their interior controls.

QUANTITY AND COMPLEXITY

These aspects often go hand-in-hand, because there are two main directions to take. If you employ fewer controls in a vehicle, the fewer controls tend to take on several functions and are more complex to use. Conversely, a larger quantity of controls can each individually be simpler to use, but then you have more options to consider from a visual standpoint. As web site and application interface designers, we deal with similar issues.

Use these examples to start taking in the large world of mobile interface design that lies beyond glowing desktop, laptop, and mobile device screens. As you do so, you can take some cues about how to best design for our mobile web experiences. What follows are some useful mobile interface guidelines and how to design and develop them.

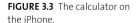

FIGURE 3.3 The calculator on the iPhone.

Whether you prefer iOS, Android, or other devices, any objective mobile customer or designer would have to agree that Apple has done a great job of setting standards for mobile interfaces. In fact, one of my colleagues who is an Android developer uses Apple's Human Interface Guidelines (HIGs) for most of his work; Google simply has not done nearly as much research and development in this area, leaving Apple as the leader.

But before you get some tips from their official guidelines, how about looking at what they have designed themselves for small screens to see how it's done? Let's take a quick look at three of Apple's iOS apps that come on the iPhone to get some design cues for designing mobile web interfaces.

CALCULATOR

The Calculator iOS app (**Figure 3.3**) is a nice example of logical, usable, and finetuned mobile interface design. So it's a great starting point for learning what to do with mobile web user interfaces.

Josh Clark, author of *Tapworthy: Designing Great iPhone Apps*, agrees. He uses Calculator as one of his examples to demonstrate that Apple often works with the magic number *44 pixels* in this and many of its user interface designs (because an average fingertip is about 44 x 44 pixels). Josh suggests that whenever possible, we should make the buttons—or any tappable areas—of our mobile interfaces at least 44 pixels in height and width (on a 320 x 480 pixel screen). I concur.

FIGURE 3.4 (left) Phone on iPhone.

FIGURE 3.5 (right) iPod on iPhone.

PHONE

In Apple's Phone app (**Figure 3.4**), however, we see something else happening that we should keep in mind. Here, the short dimension of the buttons on the keypad is 66 pixels tall; these generously-sized buttons are also 104 pixels wide.

So Apple's designers didn't just make the buttons the minimum 44 pixels and space them out more. Rather, they took advantage of the space that they had and made the buttons larger. So whenever possible, we might want to do the same and allow our mobile interfaces to grow into the space that is available.

Because, somewhat ironically, bigger is better in mobile design.

iPOD

Finally, the iPod interface (**Figure 3.5**) is a good example of using a table view navigation to list the songs in an album. Each row in the table view is a button, and is easy to tap because it is the full width of the screen.

These rows are 42 pixels tall—just a bit shy of the usual 44 that Apple uses in a lot of their layout grids. But because of their full-screen width, they can get away with them being a bit shorter.

FIGURE 3.6 The Design in Finland web site after resetting the div widths, but before doing any navigation redesign.

With some examples in our back pocket, now it's time to return our attention to our web site. In the desktop version of the Design in Finland web site, the navigation items are positioned horizontally across the top of the screen. This works great on a large screen, but certainly doesn't work well in a small mobile context.

Furthermore, despite mobilizing our screen layout in Chapter 2, the navigation improved very little. It actually became pretty jumbled up (**Figure 3.6**).

To start mobilizing the navigation, let's take a look at the HTML.

HTML

So here is the HTML markup for this site's page navigation:

```
<div class="span-24 top last" id="nav">
<ul class="main">
    <li><a href="about.html">About Design in Finland</a></li>
    <li><a href="interviews.html">Designer Interviews</a></li>
    <li><a href="map.html">Itinerary</a></li>
    <li><a href="info.html">More Information</a></li>
</ul>
</div>
```

Note that the `div` for the nav uses a Blueprint CSS grid class to define the nav area as span-24. The Blueprint grid is 24 columns wide, so this specification makes nav a full 950 pixels wide in the framework's fixed-width grid.

CSS

Next, here is the CSS that governs the layout and behavior of the original navigation:

```css
#nav {
    display: block;
}
#nav ul {
    position: static;
    list-style-type: none;
    line-height: 36px;
    overflow: hidden;
    float: none;
}
#nav li {
    float: left;
    font-size: 14px;
}
#nav a {
    margin: 0 0.5em 0 0;
    display: block;
    padding: 10px 10px 19px 10px;
    color: #555;
    font-weight: bold;
    border-bottom: none;
}
```

```
#nav a:hover, #nav a:focus {

    color: #000;

    text-decoration: underline;

}
```

The CSS rules are quite simple. They govern the layout of the list items, or buttons, so that they are laid out horizontally across the navigation area.

The trouble is, the web site does not work so well in Mobile Safari; the navigation, in particular, is illegible at first. If we adjust the content to be full-width, the horizontal navigation falls to pieces. We need something better and, preferably, something familiar. Maybe even pretty, if we can be so ambitious!

I suggest we change the navigation from horizontal to vertical (or stacked) rows. We can size and position the rows to be large and easy to tap, so we are learning from the car interfaces that we looked at earlier. And we can adjust the typography to make it as easy to read as a Swiss watch. Finally, it should be a relatively familiar navigation design, too—not all that different from what we see in Apple's own iPod app.

And to top it all off, we'll even throw in a bit of CSS3 background gradient to make the new mobile buttons beautiful.

Yes, we can be that ambitious!

MOBILE CSS

Now that we have a general specification for this new mobile navigation, what are the new style specifications for making it work in a browser?

Here are the new styles in mobile.css that I've designed for the mobile navigation:

```
#nav ul {

    width: 100%;

    padding: 0;

    margin-top: 30px;

    margin-right: 0;

    margin-bottom: 0;

    margin-left: 0;

}
```

```
#nav li {
    width: 100%;
    margin: 0;
    font-size: 14pt;
}
#nav a {
    line-height: 2.4em;
    width: auto;
    float: none;
    margin: 0;
    padding-top: 0;
    padding-right: 20px;
    padding-bottom: 0;
    padding-left: 20px;
    border-bottom-width: 1px;
    border-bottom-style: solid;
    border-bottom-color: #666;
    background-image: -webkit-gradient(
    linear,
    left bottom,
    left top,
    color-stop(0, rgb(158,158,158)),
    color-stop(0.50, rgb(212,212,212)),
    color-stop(0.75, rgb(235,235,235))
    );
    background-image: -moz-linear-gradient(
    center bottom,
    rgb(158,158,158) 0%,
```

```
      rgb(212,212,212) 50%,
      rgb(235,235,235) 75%
      );
}
#nav a:hover, #nav a:focus {
      text-decoration: none;
}
```

Let's review how each element has been altered:

- #nav: This div has been redefined to be 100% of the page width, and with margins and padding set to 0 (except for 30px of margin on top, to add a little breathing room between the nav and the header area above).

- #nav li: The only thing that changes here is the font size; now it is 14pt.

- #nav li a: The link within each row, or button, changes in a few ways. First, the size is set at 2.4em. This could also be set in pixels, but it's a bit easier to do in ems. Then the width is set to auto; this causes the touchable space to expand to fill the entire row. The rest of the padding and border styling give the rows a gray button appearance. Note how the background gradient is defined twice, once for Webkit-based browsers and again for Mozilla-based browsers.

- #nav li a:hover, #nav a:focus: The underline mouseover effect from the desktop style is removed.

So how does this look? Pull back the curtains! (**Figure 3.7**)
This is much better, isn't it?
Now the page title is larger, the content is larger, and the navigation is larger. But the navigation isn't just larger—it is totally redesigned. Now the navigation has links that are stacked vertically in rectangular rows, have a background gradient, and look a lot like the buttons in mobile applications like the iPod app shown in Figure 3.5.

FIGURE 3.7 The Design in Finland web site (www.mobilizingwebsites.net/finland/) when viewed in Mobile Safari on an iPhone, and now using the new mobile.css stylesheet.

And that's all there is to it. This web site now responds to mobile devices by presenting an attractive app-style navigation that is much easier to use. It's a lot easier to read, and has large buttons scaled to human fingers. No more pinching or zooming is required to navigate this web site.

WRAPPING **UP**

Without a lot of modification, a grid-based, fixed-width web site can have its navigation substantially improved for mobile presentation and context. You learned from examining some familiar mobile apps that a minimum of 44 pixels in height and width is a good size for a navigation button. You also saw that when space is available to make a button larger, you should do so—larger is generally better. Finally, the visual style of a mobile navigation does not need to match the original. In this case, you updated the navigation to be responsive to mobile screens, changing from a horizontal layout with a mouseover effect to having a vertical layout with an appearance more suitable for mobile use.

See, optimizing a web site for mobile use isn't so hard, is it?

4

MOBILIZING
IMAGES

Images have been making our communications and storytelling come
alive since cave drawing, oil painting, and photography. What
are some considerations and techniques for images in mobile
web presentation?

A **HOLISTIC APPROACH** TO **MOBILE IMAGES**

With digital photography and illustration, especially on the web, we have been increasingly accustomed to our CSS-empowered browsers gracefully processing image placement and scaling. And now with CSS3, the options keep growing to include fancy border treatments, more sophisticated layout options, and more.

So in modern browsers, we might expect the transition from desktop to mobile to be similarly magical and trouble-free. And, in many respects, it can go pretty darn well. But mobilizing images is about more than the technical details and relying on the browser to do everything. Let's examine some design considerations, along with their technical solutions, so that you can approach mobilizing images in a holistic manner.

INLINE IMAGES

When it comes to mobile images, you might initially jump to the conclusion that images should always be smaller because the screens are smaller, so therefore the images should take up less of that precious real estate.

Which can be true in some cases. But not always!

SOMETIMES MOBILIZING MEANS SMALLER ...

As Figure 3.7 illustrated at the end of the previous chapter, one of the issues you can run into is an image that was originally sized to display at its full size. Consider the blue and white Finnish flag at the top of the screen as an example of this. It is 150 pixels wide and 90 pixels tall. For the original 950 pixel wide design of the desktop experience, this flag was sized in Photoshop and intended to be displayed at 100%.

So the CSS for this image in `main.css` is:

```
img#flag {
    margin-right: 15px;
    border: 1px solid #999;
}
```

Granted, there are two issues going on in this area of the design at the moment: a flag image that may be too large, and the "Design in Finland" text that is also too large for the space of the small screen. We will deal just with the image issue here.

The solution for the image, as you have probably guessed, is to size it down a bit. Fortunately, our HTML allows us to do this rather conveniently:

```
<img src="../images/flag.png" alt="Finnish flag" id="flag" />
```

Note that there are no width or height attributes in the `img` tag. And this is exactly what we want when we are relying on CSS to do the heavy lifting of styling and positioning—keep the HTML light and airy, providing just a touch of structure to our content.

So note that if you have `img` tags with width and height attributes, and you're striving for a responsive, mobilized design, you will want to strip out those attributes and have your CSS do the sizing; set an id or class for each image as you do this.

FIGURE 4.1 Our resized Finnish flag, no longer dominating the header with its full glory of 150 pixel width.

Getting back to resizing the image, adding a new CSS rule in `mobile.css` for this image looks like this:

```
img#flag {
    width: 25%;
    margin-top: 20px;
}
```

The adjustments include narrowing the width to 25% which, on a mobile screen of 320 pixels, results in a more modest flag that is 38 pixels wide instead of 150. I also added a margin of 20px above the flag. Previously, it was flush to the top of the page and looked a bit goofy in the mobile presentation.

But other than that, I'm taking advantage of the cascading nature of CSS and not redefining the border or right margin of the flag in `main.css`. Consequently, those properties are still applied to the flag and the result is a flag with a narrow gray border and some right margin to buffer the headline text, just as before (**Figure 4.1**).

Perfect!

FIGURE 4.2 The interview page when viewed in the desktop version of Safari.

... AND SOMETIMES MOBILIZING MEANS LARGER

In other cases, you may not want to use your images at 100% or even size them smaller. There are cases where you will want to size them larger instead.

Seriously? Make them bigger when you have less screen to work with?

Yes. Seriously.

To see why, let's take a look at the images in the interview section of the Finnish design web site (**Figure 4.2**). In a desktop environment, they have been sized to be adjacent to each other. This layout is attractive and works quite well, and the image size (40% of their 600 pixel width) is just right for showing detail.

FIGURE 4.3 The interview page when viewed in the mobile version of Safari.

But when viewing this page on a mobile screen (**Figure 4.3**), I feel that the images are kind of small. The layout itself is still fine, but if I want to emphasize the images as content, I'm not certain that it's particularly successful here.

So the lesson here isn't nearly as technical as it is contextual and editorial: if you are assessing the success of images in mobile presentation, don't hesitate to make them *larger* to make them work better on *smaller* screens.

In this case, the adjustment to make in the CSS is fairly simple, going from this in main.css:

```
.interviewphotos img {
    width: 40%;
    padding: 10px;
}
```

to these additional rules in mobile.css:

```
.interviewphotos {
    width: 100%;
}
.interviewphotos img {
    width: 90%;
}
```

Vesa Loikas, Architect and Graphic Designer
Turku

Vesa Loikas discussed Finnish design primarily from the standpoint of architecture. After living and working in the United States for ten years, he has a unique perspective on Finland—that of

FIGURE 4.4 (left) The interview page when viewed in the mobile version of Safari.

FIGURE 4.5 (right) As you scroll the interview page in mobile Safari, the larger images are still manageable. There's more scrolling, to be sure—but it is still reasonable.

These changes do two essential things:

1. The change to the `interviewphotos` class makes the div's width 100% of the screen width.

2. The change to any images contained in an `interviewphotos` div results in them being 90% of the div width (or 90% of the screen width).

The redefinition of `interviewphotos` and `interviewphotos img` results in this mobile presentation of the images as shown in **Figure 4.4**.

Granted, the photos stack now and increase scrolling. Might too much of this be a problem on a mobile device? It certainly could—I'm not suggesting that stacking everything works in every case, so you have to make your own judgment calls on a project-by-project (and even screen-by-screen) basis. But the scrolling in this example is not outrageous by any means, and as you go from image to image, the text beneath the images resumes and keeps prodding the user to scroll. It's a natural flow that is aesthetically and contextually pleasing (**Figure 4.5**).

So we have examined two ways to handle inline images. Deciding when to make something smaller or when to make something larger is a decision to make based on the amount and purpose of your image content.

FIGURE 4.6 A photo gallery using CSS3 columns. Living in the future!

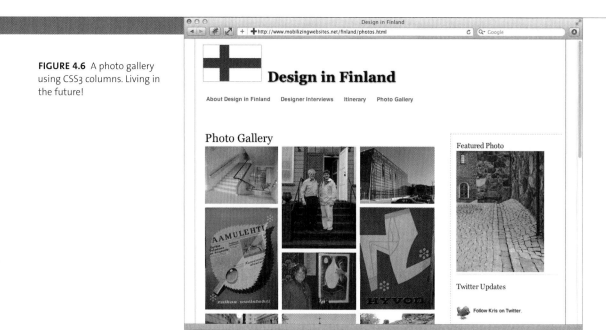

There are a variety of techniques for integrating photos and other images into web sites, and among them are some cool techniques for making larger image layouts responsive.

The responsive photo grid used in Design for Finland's Photo Gallery uses two fantastic CSS3 properties, `column-count` and `column-gap`. These are properties that have support in some of the most popular browsers (Firefox, Safari, Opera) and, notably, in their mobile offspring.

So first, let's take a look at what this photo grid looks like in a regular desktop browser. The idea is to tile photos and have them flow through a series of columns from left to right across the page. The approach is based on how newspaper and magazine columns work in print: when a column fills, the flow moves over one column to the right and automatically starts filling the next column. **Figure 4.6** shows the result with 20 photos.

One of the techniques that I particularly like is demonstrated by the fine web craftsperson Chris Coyier (http://chriscoyier.net). To learn more about how this is implemented, visit http://css-tricks.com/13372-seamless-responsive-photo-grid/.

So yeah, it looks suspiciously like a table doing the work here, doesn't it? Well don't you dare accuse me of something so gauche! There's just the tiniest of clues in the HTML that points to what is going on:

```
<div id="grid">

<img src="images/gridimages/01.jpg" alt="Paimio Hospital, Alvar
→ Aalto" />

<img src="images/gridimages/02.jpg" alt="Poster design, Erik Bruun" />

<img src="images/gridimages/03.jpg" alt="Bench, Helsinki" />

<img src="images/gridimages/04.jpg" alt="Old home, Turku" />

<img src="images/gridimages/05.jpg" alt="Cathedral, Turku" />

<img src="images/gridimages/06.jpg" alt="Bruun home, Suomenlinna" />

...

</div>
```

That's right, other than a series of img tags, there is nothing to the HTML markup at all—just the div id.

So what does the CSS look like? Well, like this in the site's main.css file:

```
#grid {
    line-height: 0;
    -webkit-column-count: 3;
    -webkit-column-gap: 10px;
    -moz-column-count: 3;
    -moz-column-gap: 10px;
    column-count: 3;
    column-gap: 10px;
}
```

```
#grid img {
    width: 100% !important;
    height: auto !important;
    margin-bottom: 10px;
}
```

Wow, that's it? Indeed—sometimes this great CSS3 stuff is as magical as it looks!

All you need to do is use the three flavors of `column-count` as one needs to with any CSS3 property these days, to cover yourself for both WebKit and Mozilla browsers, as well as to future-proof your CSS when browser prefixes are no longer necessary.

Then, you just define a spacer using `column-gap` if you do not want the images to be flush against each other. This takes care of the behavior for the `div` that wraps the images, `#grid`. Then for any image located inside the `div`, the width is specified to be 100%, the height auto, and each image has a 10 pixel margin below it to match the 10 pixel gap in between the columns.

How does this respond to mobile browsers? Here's a wonderful lesson to savor from this use of CSS3: the easier it is to define a behavior in CSS, the easier it is to modify it for mobile responsiveness.

So hold on to your hat, because all you need to do is throw in a few media queries to have this layout respond to smaller screens. For the case study web site, I have chosen two different responses, one for screens 320px or smaller and another for screens up to 480px. Here's what you add to `mobile.css`:

```
@media (max-width: 480px) {
    #grid {
    -moz-column-count: 2;
    -webkit-column-count: 2;
    column-count: 2;
    }
}
```

FIGURE 4.7 The responsive photo grid in portrait orientation as viewed in Mobile Safari.

FIGURE 4.8 The same responsive photo grid in landscape orientation.

```
@media (max-width: 320px) {

    #grid {

    -moz-column-count: 1;

    -webkit-column-count: 1;

    column-count: 1;

    }

}
```

Adding this to the site's `mobile.css` file does some quick and dirty magic, reducing the photo grid to two columns at 480 pixels or smaller (the size of the iPhone screen in landscape orientation) and to a single column at 320 pixels or smaller (and if you want to be more specific about targeting more specific screen sizes, adjust your media query accordingly).

So let's take a look at the mobile versions of this flexible photo grid in **Figures 4.7** and **4.8**.

I just love the simplicity of this responsive grid, and I feel like I could experiment for hours optimizing layouts for specific ranges of screen sizes (but I'll let you take it further if you wish!). And I am also a huge fan of the asymmetrical layouts that can result by interspersing landscape- and portrait-oriented images in this layout—I think the results can be really beautiful.

So continue to have fun with image layouts in your web sites, and do not feel constrained by mobile presentations of your images. A design constraint is just another name for a design opportunity!

WRAPPING **UP**

Optimizing the presentation of images on mobile devices can be done with the right application of CSS properties. Sometimes merely resorting to tried and true CSS2 properties in the case of resizing inline images or their container divs will do the trick. And in the case of using a flexible image grid, the extra magic that CSS3 can leverage makes the work (and the results) even more fun and responsive.

But do not let the two examples in this chapter suggest that these are the only directions to take. This case study is meant to be more than instructional—I hope it's also inspirational. Please take mobilization further in your own designs. Experiment with CSS in ways that allow your specific web site to respond to mobile conditions in the ways that it was meant to, way back when it was first designed!

5

MOBILIZING **TEXT**

By now you're probably getting tired of seeing the jumbo, poorly-sized text heading that keeps shouting "Design in! Finland!" at you. After all, text is an essential component of any web site. And for many sites, text is the primary content. So how do we mobilize text?

TAKE A **USER-CENTERED** APPROACH TO **MOBILIZING TEXT**

Interesting—it's taken us until Chapter 5 to get around to dealing directly with text for mobile presentation. Am I crazy? Is text so unimportant?

Of course not (on both counts). Text is incredibly important, and the chapter order does not imply that it's either less important or should only be dealt with after completely fine-tuning layout and images.

But the book needed chapters (publishers and editors can come up with the *craziest* requirements!), so I chose to address mobile in bite-sized pieces and by topic. Otherwise, if this book were organized like a real design project, it would have one chapter entitled "How to optimize layout, navigation, images, and text, all at the same time and also jump from one to the other. A lot."

So if you're thinking, "Hmm, I could very well be adjusting my text, images, and layout ALL AT THE SAME TIME," rest assured, you are not engaging in crazy talk. Ideally, your mobilizing workflow—after a round of isolating and practicing techniques in this manner—will become more holistic, and you will indeed be adjusting all aspects of your design more concurrently.

Anyway, thanks for being patient as this case study continues to reveal itself. And let's move on to dealing directly with that text!

BY WHICH **MEASURE**: A **POINT** OR AN **em**?

As we start to contemplate having our text resize itself for mobile presentation, we need to consider units and measures. Which will work for us? Any of them? Let's find out.

HEADING

When working in mobile, I happen to have a personal preference for using points as the measure. The reasons are simple: points allow me to more quickly and granularly size within the smaller confines of mobile screens, and I find points easier to work with when developing a system of relative type sizes. Let's see how this works.

Starting with the over-sized page title "Design in Finland," here is how it was coded in HTML:

```
<h1><a href="index.html"><img src="images/flag.png"
alt="Finnish flag" id="flag" />Design in Finland</a></h1>
```

As we typically do, I wrapped the top-level heading of the site's pages in h1 tags. To style it in main.css, this is what I did:

```
h1 {
    font-size: 3em;
    margin: 0px;
    padding: 0px 0px 0px 20px;
    text-shadow: 1px 1px 3px #333;
}
```

For the desktop browser experience, I took the best path at the time and used em for the unit instead of point. We are familiar with the reasons why: ems allow you to scale your text sizes relatively, so this is more flexible than using a fixed unit. And in older browsers, it was also easier for people to resize type that was set in ems. But nowadays, modern browsers scale the entire page—largely to maintain line length and layout integrity. So em is not as important as it used to be, at least for accessibility reasons.

FIGURE 5.1 The title "Design in Finland" resized to 16pt in the mobile stylesheet.

So I find that using em isn't as necessary now, and prefer to instead take advantage of the level of control that using points affords me. So for the new mobile size for h1, I adjusted the point size by one point at a time until I arrived at a new size for my mobile.css:

```
h1 {
font-size: 16pt;
}
```

And the result is shown in **Figure 5.1**.

BODY CONTENT: PARAGRAPHS

Now let's move on to the main body text (we will return to other typographic details like subheadings next). The p tags in main.css were also sized using the scalable em unit:

```
p {
    font-size: 1.4em;
    line-height: 1.6em;
}
```

Tervetuloa!

This web site represents my experience of researching design in Finland and, specifically, how that country's culture, sense of place, and affinity for nature influence Finnish design. This research took place in May 2002 as part of my thesis project for my Master of Fine Arts degree in interactive design.

My thesis project began with an interview phase in which I traveled to Finland for 10 days to meet with Finnish designers and design

Tervetuloa!

This web site represents my experience of researching design in Finland and, specifically, how that country's culture, sense of place, and affinity for nature influence Finnish design. This research took place in May 2002 as part of my thesis project for my Master of Fine Arts degree in interactive design.

My thesis project began with an interview phase in which I traveled to Finland for 10 days to meet with Finnish designers and design curators, educators, and marketers. Interviews were digitally recorded for later use in the design project, and digital photography was also collected to visually document the discovery experience.

FIGURE 5.2 (left) The introductory paragraphs for "Design in Finland" sized at 1.4em.

FIGURE 5.3 (right) The introductory paragraphs for "Design in Finland" sized at 11pt.

This size ended up working quite well for the desktop browser presentation of the site when it was first designed because it resulted in a line length of approximately 75 characters. This is at the end of the acceptable range of what Robert Bringhurst, author of *The Elements of Typographic Style*, recommends for optimal readability, which is 45–75 characters per line.

But when viewed in Mobile Safari (**Figure 5.2**), this 1.4em font size looks a bit chunky to me. And it's only around 35 characters per line, so it falls below the recommended range.

So to more granularly control text size, I am going to continue to march ahead with point sizing in `mobile.css`:

```
p {
    font-size: 11pt;
    line-height: 15pt;
}
```

This is now looking better (**Figure 5.3**).

However, I note that the line length only crept up to about 40 characters per line. That's just under the 45–75 characters per line that most people aim for in print and web typography.

So here's an important lesson: recommended line lengths do not need to be as religiously observed for mobile presentation. If we went with a more typical line length in mobile, we would simply be moving backwards to a typical desktop presentation crammed into a mobile browser. That is exactly what we're trying to avoid in this exercise!

Therefore, I recommend being comfortable with line lengths that go down to 40 characters per line for regular paragraph text in mobile. And note that I'm still giving it some breathing room with a 15pt line height. Do not skimp on line height by trying to cram too much onto the screen. As Figure 5.3 showed, we're still gaining about 3–4 lines of text in portrait orientation as compared to our original larger size.

BODY CONTENT: SUBHEADINGS

Finally, let's take a quick look at the subheadings on each page. The h2 tags, used as page titles, were sized using the scalable em unit in main.css, as were the h3 tags used as section headings:

```
h2 {
    font-size: 2.2em;
}
h3 {
    font-size: 1.8em;
    line-height: 1.6em;
}
```

And **Figure 5.4** shows the mobile presentation.

As expected, I am not quite happy with this presentation and would like to see if it can be tweaked just a bit. My preference is to go slightly smaller in both subheadings and also distinguish them a bit more by type weight. Am I making up for deficiencies in the original design? Perhaps. So yeah, do not hesitate to use what you learn in mobilizing a web site to also improve your desktop presentation.

FIGURE 5.4 (left) The subheading and section heading sized in ems.

FIGURE 5.5 (right) The subheading and section heading sized in points.

After throwing these details back into the design lab for some more R&D, here's what I arrived at for my new subheading and section type specifications in `mobile.css`:

```
h2 {
    font-size: 14pt;
    font-weight: bold;
}
h3 {
    font-size: 13pt;
    font-style: italic;
}
```

And **Figure 5.5** shows the results rendered in Mobile Safari.

The point of this exercise is not to be overly prescriptive with particular type sizes for mobile. You may decide to be much more granular than this, for example, and specify additional sizes for additional screen sizes. What I do emphasize, as I already mentioned, is not to apply the same typographic specifications you may be familiar with from print and web to the mobile screen. Line character lengths definitely need to be a bit lower, and how you differentiate information in your hierarchy may lead to new mobile styles.

FIGURE 5.6 The full-size presentation of Wikipedia.

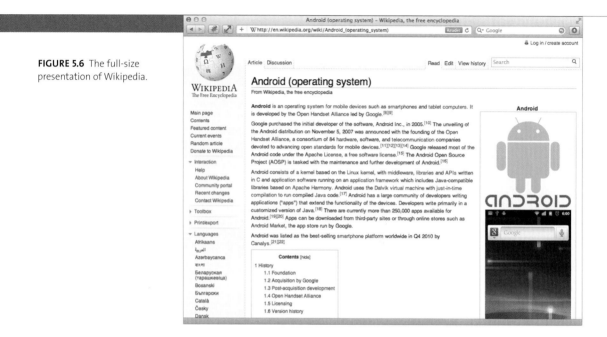

To move on to another issue and technique for dealing with text in the mobile context: what about the issue of *quantity*? Isn't it true that many web sites simply have way too much content to conveniently present in a mobile context? How can one deal with that?

An approach I will cover next is inspired by a web site that we are all familiar with, Wikipedia. And while Wikipedia does not employ a responsive approach to the mobile web (they choose to redirect visitors to a separate mobile web site), I still think it's helpful to learn from their presentation techniques and explore how they handle large quantities of text. I mean, it's an *encyclopedia*, for goodness sake. Let's learn from the most extreme, verbose example we can find!

Wikipedia's approach to mobilizing web content, and making it easier to absorb all of the text that can be in an article, is to spoon-feed it in small, bite-sized, quantities.

And this is an approach that can work very well for any long pages that we might be dealing with, so let's take a look at how one can responsively break up content in this manner. Because if it works for Wikipedia, it has to work for everyone else, too.

First, let's take a look at the results of Wikipedia's approach. I looked up the Android mobile operating system in Wikipedia on my laptop, and **Figure 5.6** shows how it looks.

FIGURE 5.7 (left) The mobile presentation of Wikipedia, starting with the right column of the full-screen presentation.

FIGURE 5.8 (right) The mobile presentation of Wikipedia, proceeding with the article introduction.

Note that in the article, there are three main areas. There is the primary text area that begins under the article title. It features the introduction to the topic and, as it does here, often goes on for just a couple of paragraphs.

In the right-hand column is a narrower presentation in summary format. For people, this includes basic biographical information. For countries, things like the capital city, population, and such. And for Android, it displays comparable statistics like the owner, program, initial release, and so on. Pay particular attention to this column in the desktop version (as something interesting happens to it in mobile).

Finally, back in the main column and under the introduction is the third main element of a Wikipedia article: the table of contents. Pay particular attention to this, too. It is with the right-hand column and table of contents that Wikipedia does something quite practical within its mobile presentation.

So let's take a peek at Wikipedia's mobile presentation next (**Figure 5.7**).

Do you notice anything interesting? I sure do! The beginning of the article in mobile is the same narrow right-hand column from the regular full-screen layout. *It looks exactly the same.* Brilliant! And the people at Wikipedia are able to pull this off because, unless they just happened to get really lucky (doubtful), they sized the right column of the full-screen presentation to already be mobile-friendly. I'm guessing this was a great "mobile first" decision on their part. And it works wonderfully, because it makes the transition from desktop or laptop to mobile that much more seamless.

Next comes the article introduction (**Figure 5.8**).

FIGURE 5.9 (left) The mobile presentation of a Wikipedia article's table of contents.

FIGURE 5.10 (right) The article's table of contents with the first section opened.

Nothing particularly special here—just the same introduction as in the regular presentation, sized right for the mobile context. So it requires quite a bit more scrolling to read, but not a big problem, really. And I also note that Wikipedia uses line lengths in the 40–50 character range for its paragraph text, so that verifies what we were aiming for earlier in this chapter.

But now is where it gets more interesting. Let's take a look at what follows (**Figure 5.9**).

Below the article introduction is the table of contents—except now it is presented differently! Instead of links to page anchors like in the full-screen presentation, the rest of the article has been compacted, concealed, and neatly packaged into an accordion-style presentation. Each section can now be expanded and revealed, one at a time, by tapping the Show button. If you want to manage the presentation of the article by keeping the revealed content to a minimum, you can conceal it again by tapping Hide. This allows people to read the article section by section with a lot less scrolling, and lot more direct control of the experience (**Figure 5.10**).

What a great way to present a mountain of content in a mobile context!

So how is it done? And, more importantly for the purposes of this book, how much work does it take to inject this technique into an existing web site?

Let's take a look at that next. I promise you will be pleasantly surprised!

HTML

There are a few alterations to your HTML that are required when employing this technique, but they are pretty minimal.

The primary change is to wrap each content section that you want to initially hide with the highlighted text below:

```
<h3 class="section_heading" id="section_1"><button class=
    "section_heading show" section_id="1">Show</button>
    <button class="section_heading hide"
    section_id="1">Hide</button>Erik Bruun</h3>
<div class="content_block" id="content_1">

<h3 id="bruun">Erik Bruun, Graphic Designer and
→ Illustrator<br>Helsinki</h3>

<div class="interviewphotos"><img src="images/bruun1.jpg" alt="Erik
→ Bruun."><img src="images/bruun2.jpg" alt="Erik's tools."></div>

<p>Much of Erik Bruun's work has nature themes, and is the result of a
→ conscious effort on his part to raise society's consciousness
→ of...

...Similarly, when friends from elsewhere in Europe visit him and
→ he takes them to his summer cottage on a lake, they do not
→ understand his interest in being there and ask if he ever is
→ afraid of being alone.</p>

<p><a href="#bodycontent" class="returnnav">return to top of
→ page</a></p>

</div>
```

The new code at work is an h3-level header area for each section that includes the Show and Hide buttons. This header precedes a new `div` that wraps the section of content to be hidden and revealed. As long as the `id` of the new header area matches the `id` of the content_block `div`, the buttons will operate accordingly and do their work.

So is this the only HTML change? Not quite. And how does this new HTML do its magic, anyway? The answer to both questions lies in three more lines of code in the head of the page:

```
<link href="css/collapse.css" rel="stylesheet" type="text/css" />
<script type="text/javascript" src="js/jquery-1.2.6.js"></script>
<script type="text/javascript" src="js/collapse.js"></script>
```

This shouldn't come as a surprise: the show/hide effect is both appearance and behavior, so this needs to involve CSS for the former and JavaScript for the latter.

CSS

The new collapse.css file is not particularly long or complicated. Let's take a look:

```
h3.section_heading {display: none;}
.content_block {display: inline;}
@media (max-width: 480px) {
    #secondarynav {
        display: none;
    }
    h3.section_heading {
        display: block;
        font-size: 13pt;
        text-align: left;
        font-weight: bold;
        height: 1.8em;
```

```
        padding: 0;
        margin: 0px 0px 5px 0px;
    }
    button {
        font-size: .75em;
    }
    .content_block, button.section_heading.hide {
        display: none;
    }
}
```

The first two lines set the default desktop browser appearance for the two new elements in our HTML: don't display the new show/hide navigation, but display all of the content. That way the page appears exactly as it did in a desktop browser, as if you didn't make any of these code changes at all.

But then the media query kicks in nicely, specifying that under 480 pixels of width, something different happens: do not display the normal jump navigation (#secondarynav), display the new show/hide element that is wrapped in h3.sectionheading, and hide the content in the .content_block section until the user taps on Show.

That leads us to the final part of this technique: the behavior.

JAVASCRIPT

As previously noted, there are two lines that link to JavaScript files. One pulls in a version of the jQuery JavaScript library and another pulls in a JavaScript file based on an earlier version of Wikipedia's mobile site (the current beta version of Wikipedia mobile looks and behaves the same, but uses newer code than this example).

I'll be the first person to tell you that I couldn't write a line of JavaScript from scratch to save my life, so don't expect to see the JavaScript explained in detail here; Jedi-level JavaScript work is beyond the scope of this book. So I use existing JavaScript libraries and files for the same reason that most visual web designers use them: they make us look brilliant, and save us from a lot of programming angst!

FIGURE 5.11 (left) A second version of the Designer Interviews mobile screen (http://www.mobilizingwebsites.net/finland/interviews2.html) employing the show and hide technique.

FIGURE 5.12 (right) The second version of the Designer Interviews mobile screen after tapping on Show, revealing that section of content.

But if you're JavaScript-savvy, by all means, take a look at the files. And if you wish to employ a newer version of jQuery or any other fine collection of JavaScript library behaviors, please do so—this example is but one version of how to solve a show/hide behavior with JavaScript and CSS.

In a nutshell, however, the Show and Hide buttons need JavaScript as the glue to instruct the content area to reveal and hide itself when the buttons are tapped. Therein lay the directions to make this happen, as the effect is more than just appearance—it's also behavior that changes the appearance. Something that Java-Script is exceedingly good at. Thanks, JavaScript!

So what are the results of this technique when applied to the interviews screen of the Design in Finland web site? **Figure 5.11** shows what we see now in the mobile presentation.

And **Figure 5.12** shows how it looks after tapping on Show.

It works great! And I hope you are pleasantly surprised like I predicted—it does not take rocket science to pull it off.

WRAPPING **UP**

Mobilizing content can happen at dramatically different levels. We can size and style text with new typographic rules that better support the mobile context. We can also reveal content in bite-sized pieces to reduce the need to scroll through an enormously long page, all at once on a miniature screen. Regardless of where you begin, I hope this chapter helps you take a closer look at the text content in your web sites and make better choices about how you can incrementally mobilize it without a radical redesign or rewrite.

Project Interview 2

The **Boston Globe**

I had started hearing about it in 2010
when An Event Apart was in Minneapolis,
and Ethan Marcotte gave a presentation about responsive web
design. And then when it launched in fall 2011, The Boston Globe
responsive redesign became the talk of the web standards com-
munity. It was one of the first responsive redesigns of a large web
site for a general readership.

FIGURE PI 2.1 (above) The new Boston Globe home page in a desktop browser.

FIGURE PI 2.2 (right) The new Boston Globe home page in a mobile browser.

Also unique to the project: The Boston Globe *sought out* responsive design as part of their redesign solution, and *touts it as a hallmark feature*. They even have a special Features section to highlight how it works, to help readers become aware of this approach to content delivery in different contexts and understand how it works (see **Figures PI 2.3** and **PI 2.4**).

Once the site went live, I was impressed and inspired. So I went directly to Ethan Marcotte, the source of much of the design innovation that shaped this responsive design, to see if he would have some time to tell us more about the project.

The author of *Responsive Web Design (A Book Apart)*, an independent design consultant, and a popular speaker on the web conference circuit, Ethan has a lot on his plate. So I was grateful for his willingness to participate in the following interview. Thanks so much, Ethan!

FIGURE PI 2.3 (left) The Features section of The Boston Globe in a desktop browser.

FIGURE PI 2.4 (right) The Features section of The Boston Globe in a mobile browser.

WHAT WAS YOUR ROLE IN DESIGNING THE
NEW BOSTON GLOBE WEB SITE?

I was hired by Filament Group, a design firm based in Boston. They had been brought on by the Globe to create a finished, responsive site from an approved design. The Globe had also hired Upstatement, another Boston-based studio, to tackle the creative direction for the site.

My role was largely focused on working with Filament on matters of interaction design—of realizing the finished mockups in HTML/CSS, and then tackling larger issues of interface. I also helped establish a process for creating a responsive site of this scale.

FOLLOWING UP ON THAT, HOW WAS SCALE A FACTOR IN THIS REDESIGN?

While I wouldn't say that "scale" was a major design consideration per se, it was an important one. It absolutely influenced our thinking about the site's front-end architecture, as we invested a lot of time focused on asset management: testing for features in your browser or device, and loading CSS or JavaScript conditionally (you know, good old progressive enhancement!). Now, some folks might say that this is basically the cost of doing business with a responsive site—that when you're delivering one HTML document to every device, you need to be careful with what files you're delivering. I'd agree, but I'd add that these are practices I'd apply to any site, responsive or not.

Beyond the technical bits, much of our work revolved around establishing a more collaborative design process between Upstatement, Filament, and the Globe. Early on we realized that a more nimble, iterative process for producing the pages was key, as a set of fixed, inflexible mockups can't easily communicate how a page will render on a phone, tablet, or a widescreen display. So continuing the design work in HTML and CSS—with frequent visual refinement as needed—allowed us to evaluate our initial design assumptions in the browsers and devices that our audience would be viewing our work in.

SO THE CLIENT PLANNED ON DESIGNING RESPONSIVELY?
THAT SOUNDS PRETTY LEADING-EDGE FOR A CLIENT!

Yes, the Globe was already committed to a responsive approach by the time I came on board, which was pretty exciting to hear. They were—and still are—committed to as broad a level of access as possible, and a responsive approach paired beautifully with that goal.

WHAT WAS THE BIGGEST DESIGN CHALLENGE IN THIS PROJECT?

It might not look like it, but the masthead is probably the most complicated part of the design. We iterated the design a number of times, and came to the current solution through a sizable amount of collaborative design sessions between Filament, the Globe, Upstatement, and myself.

DO YOU HAVE A FAVORITE SECTION OF THE NEW SITE THAT YOU THINK WORKS PARTICULARLY WELL FOR MOBILE?

That's a hard one—not least because I think my answer would probably change if you asked me again in a few days' time. From a visual standpoint, I think the Magazine is probably one of my favorites. The layout feels fairly rich on a desktop, but we were all really happy with how accessible it still felt on a phone or a tablet (see **Figures PI 2.5** and **PI 2.6**).

From a technical standpoint, I think the My Saved feature is pretty fantastic. It's accessible on JavaScript-free interfaces from individual articles, but enhances up to a fairly cool UI on more robust devices. On touch displays, you can actually toggle a "save" mode on the home page and section fronts by using a two-finger

FIGURE PI 2.5 (left) The Boston Globe Magazine section in a desktop browser.

FIGURE PI 2.6 (right) The Boston Globe Magazine section in a mobile browser.

tap. I should also mention that the folks at Filament Group, specifically Scott Jehl, are really responsible for how cool the interface is, and the Globe dev team did a fantastic job bringing the application to life.

WHILE EXPLORING THE BOSTON GLOBE ON DESKTOP AND MOBILE, I'M SURPRISED NOT TO NOTICE ANY CONTENT THAT IS NOT DISPLAYED IN THE MOBILE PRESENTATION. DID THE TEAM TRULY FIND A PLACE FOR EVERYTHING?

I'm really glad you picked up on that! Much of our work during the design phase was centered on ensuring that the content we were designing was valuable to *all* of the Globe's readers, regardless of their device, and avoiding the use of display: none. As a result, the design process we adopted moved quickly into prototyping: moving beyond fixed, inflexible comps, and reviewing the design live on various browsers and devices.

If a certain feature, module, or page felt too complex or unwieldy on a mobile device, we would initiate a larger discussion about that element's value for *any* of our readers. In other words, we took a lot of inspiration from Luke Wroblewski's "mobile first" mantra. Ideally, the responsive designer makes a commitment to making their content accessible across every device, every "context." Mobile first is a really effective wedge for starting that discussion: if this content is not valuable to your mobile visitors, what value does it have for *any* of your visitors?

THE GLOBE TAKES AN APPROACH OF PRESENTING STORIES IN ENTIRE SECTIONS, WHERE THE REST OF A SECTION'S STORIES ARE SUMMARIZED BENEATH THE ONE YOU'RE READING. THIS SEEMS MORE FAITHFUL TO ACTUAL NEWSPAPERS, WHERE STORIES ARE SURROUNDED BY OTHER STORIES IN A SECTION.

I really like your analogy to the paper-based experience. This lovely feature was introduced by Upstatement and with the Globe's digital creative director, Miranda Mulligan.

THERE HAS BEEN A LOT OF DISCUSSION ABOUT TECHNIQUES
FOR DEALING WITH MOBILE IMAGES. ANY TIPS BASED ON
WHAT THE BOSTON GLOBE DOES WITH IMAGES?

The responsive images script (https://github.com/filamentgroup/Responsive-Images) was one of the early by-products of the Globe design. While we can't create any correlations between the size of a device's screen and the amount of bandwidth it uses, I still feel as though the script is a very elegant solution. It defaults to a smaller image, but then enhances up to a wider one if the rendering screen is above a certain resolution threshold.

Since Filament published the script, I know that a significant number of alternate approaches have been created. Jason Grigsby has done a fantastic round-up on his blog, discussing the strengths and limitations of each (http://www.cloudfour.com/responsive-imgs/). But I think that a number of very recent changes to various browsers' preloading behavior have complicated, if not broken, some of these client-side solutions. Which is kind of a shame.

DOES A BIG PROJECT OF A LONG DURATION MEAN THAT YOU
NEED TO COMMIT TO CERTAIN TECHNIQUES OR FRAMEWORKS
EARLY IN THE PROJECT, EVEN IF BETTER TECHNIQUES ARISE
ALONG THE WAY DUE TO THE SPEED OF MOBILE INNOVATION?

I'm not sure we ever hit a situation like that during the course of this project. Part of it might have been because we fell into a collaborative, highly iterative design process, so that we could adjust our approach if an opportunity changed. Another part might have been that we had established some broad technical goals at the outset: an emphasis on universal access to the site's content via progressive enhancement, and a rich, responsive experience for a dizzying variety of screens.

As insufferably lofty as that might sound, setting those goals really helped unify the team throughout the course of the project. Speaking personally, I never felt like we had to bypass any opportunities that came up while trying to solve a particular problem. Part of what made The Boston Globe redesign so fun for me was how creative we were allowed to be throughout the project.

6

MOBILIZING **FORMS**

The flow of information through a
web site is not always one-way—web
sites often serve as a point of information exchange. And one of
the most common ways to facilitate this is using a form. What are
some considerations for making web forms more mobile-friendly?

MOBILE CAN IMPROVE THE
USER EXPERIENCE OF WEB FORMS

Forms.

Forms.

Forms!

FORMS!

I know, no matter how you say it or write it, people do not really like forms in web sites all that much. Almost every time I see a web form, I cringe at least a little.

This is certainly understandable, because web forms violate one of the main reasons that we flock to the web: we want to quickly and quietly interact with a person or organization. And more often than not, we visit web sites instead of picking up the phone to make a call. It just feels faster and more convenient and means that we don't need to have yet another conversation. In lives full of noise and conversations, the web can be a place of quiet and solitude!

But web forms violate this because:

1. They expect us to say something (or type, in this case)

2. Which then slows us down...

3. ...and makes us work a lot more than we might have expected to.

With web forms causing us so much angst, we need to pay as much attention as we can to their user experience and design.

So how do we do this for mobile presentation? Let's spend a little while checking it out.

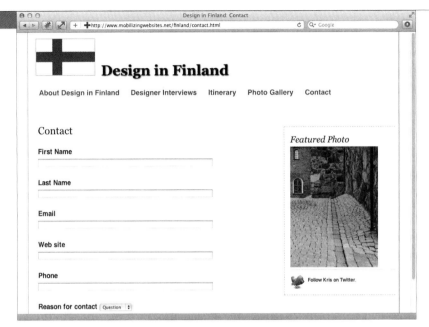

FIGURE 6.1 (left) The contact form for Design in Finland.

FIGURE 6.2 (right) The mobile version of the contact form for Design in Finland.

Let's consider the web form in Design in Finland (**Figure 6.1**).

What's interesting is, at least on the surface, the form fields all look the same. They've even been given the same width. Only the text labels are different in the desktop browser experience. And, certainly, the keyboard of your computer does not transform as you fill out such a form.

Transforming keyboard? Where did that crazy idea even come from?

From mobile.

Because on mobile, web forms become positively ingenious (**Figure 6.2**).

FIGURE 6.3 The First Name field activated in the mobile version, with the full keyboard displayed.

INPUT TYPE = "TEXT"

When looking at mobile web forms, they don't necessarily look that different. What we really need to do is start poking around a bit under the hood. For example, the essence of a form's HTML is this:

```
<form name="name" method="post" action="text">
<label>First Name<br />
<input type="text" class="formfield" name="firstname"
→  id="firstname">
</label>
<input type="submit" name="button" id="button" value="Submit">
</form>
```

And this is the starting point of the form in our case study web site. This code first specifies a form, then specifies a text field labeled First Name, establishes a Submit button, and finally closes out the form. And when you tap on the First Name field, you see what is shown in **Figure 6.3**.

And after that, it starts getting interesting!

INPUT TYPE = "EMAIL"

Remember the comment about the transforming keyboard, where you thought I must have been hallucinating a bit? Fear not, I wasn't. Keyboards can transform in mobile, and this can feel so natural that you might not even pay much attention to it when it happens.

But after tapping the Email field in this web form, you see what's shown in **Figure 6.4**.

Yes, the change is subtle, but it's also brilliant. Because what does every email address in the world have in common? An @ between the user name and domain name, and a . between the domain name and top-level domain (for example, me@you.com). So iPhone's mobile email keyboard shortens the space bar enough to make room for these characters, enabling you to type an email address without hitting shift to access the @ and . characters.

It's a contextual keyboard!

And here is the code that makes this happen:

```
<label>Email<br />
<input type="email" class="formfield" name="email" id="email">
</label>
```

HTML5 INPUT TYPES

input type = "email" and the remaining input types in this chapter are all HTML5, which is supported well in most mobile browsers. For additional information about HTML5 input types and HTML5 in general, check out Bruce Lawson's and Remy Sharp's web site *Introducing HTML5*:

http://introducinghtml5.com/

or the full HTML5 specification on the W3C web site:

http://dev.w3.org/html5/spec/Overview.html

And that is all. As long as you indicate the input type to be email, mobile devices like iPhone will serve up a keyboard that makes typing an email address easier.

FIGURE 6.5 The Web site field activated in the mobile version, with the URL keyboard displayed.

INPUT TYPE = "URL"

So if setting input type to email gets you a nice email-friendly keyboard, what are some other options? How about a responsive keyboard design for entering URLs?

Because that is also possible—as shown in **Figure 6.5**.

This is another subtle but brilliant change to the keyboard. Gone is the @ from the email keyboard. And the space bar went from long in the regular keyboard, to short in the email keyboard, to—hey, now that's gone, too!

But it's okay; there aren't any spaces in URLs.

Instead, we now have a new / and a handy .com key. And to gain these conveniences for entering a URL, this is all we need to do under the hood in our HTML:

```
<label>Web site<br />
<input type="url" class="formfield" name="web" id="web">
</label>
```

And note that in iOS, holding the .com key gives you several additional options to choose from: .net, .edu, .org, and .us. Thank you, Apple!

FIGURE 6.6 The Phone field activated in the mobile view, with the telephone keypad displayed.

INPUT TYPE = "TEL"

How about another responsive keyboard? What about one for entering phone numbers? Of course! I'm sure I don't need to tell you what happens next (**Figure 6.6**).

Truly, this is where mobile context is absolutely outstanding and ingenious. Because when we're holding a handheld device with a touchscreen, it is *not* a phone. No, not even an *iPhone* is a phone. Rather, it's a magical, transformative computer. It not only transforms how we live, *it transforms itself*. Into whatever you need for the task at hand.

In this case, everything is stripped away and recast for the job of typing in a phone number. So why not just deliver a familiar phone keypad? It not only serves up the smaller range of options needed for phone numbers, the keys are bigger. And we love the big keys on mobile devices.

Plus, the HTML to make this happen is as minimal as in our previous examples:

```
<label>Phone<br />
<input type="tel" class="formfield" name="phone" id="phone">
</label>
```

The results of designing for mobile can truly exceed those of designing for desktop. Hopefully, you will never see mobile design as being overly constraining again! Indeed, the tight constraints can yield more creative solutions.

But there's one more form option I'd like to explore.

SELECT

The mobile magic continues in other areas of web forms, too. Another fun one is the drop-down select menu.

Drop-down select menus can actually be rather tricky to use on desktops and laptops, especially if you have an equipment issue (like a sticky mouse or touchy, hypersensitive trackpad), or a physical limitation that keeps you from executing the smooth and precise movements needed to navigate through drop-down options and make your selection.

So isn't it nice that mobile once again improves on the drop-down menu? It's actually *better* on mobile.

Figure 6.7 shows how our drop-down menu is presented on the iPhone.

Apple delivers a nice pop-up controller where your options have been transformed into an animated cylinder that you roll to choose your option. It's designed a lot like a slot machine display, except that here you touch it.

And you're probably not going to win a lot of money with your selection.

Android's presentation of a drop-down form menu is different, yet equally effective (**Figure 6.8**).

Here, it's even simpler. A modal menu appears on the screen where you just tap the option you would like. Not quite as fun as Apple's, but I think the simplicity here is unrivaled. It's fantastic.

And the HTML to make this happen on mobile is absolutely unchanged from the original markup from the desktop presentation:

```
<label>Reason for contact
<select name="reason" id="reason">
    <option>Question</option>
    <option>Comment</option>
    <option>Complaint</option>
</select>
</label>
```

So here, Apple's iOS and Google's Android mobile operating systems do all of the work for you. Thanks guys!

I hope this short web forms chapter has been both encouraging and even inspirational. Truly, making your web site optimized for mobile can actually result in better experiences. And I haven't even dived into how mobile-specific styling can further enhance your web forms in a mobile presentation—I've tried to minimize any focus on pure style, to keep the book shorter as well as less about style and more about readability and usability.

FORM **LABELS**

That said, placing labels above their form fields is preferable to placing them to the left of their fields (as I've shown in these examples). The result is certainly more orderly, and fits a mobile screen much better.

Still, don't stop here: exercise your creativity by experimenting with how CSS styles can improve your mobile web forms even more!

WRAPPING **UP**

In this chapter, you learned that web forms can actually be substantially better when presented in a mobile context than on a desktop. As long as you are careful about specifying the right input type for your forms' fields, you can leverage some nice user experience enhancements that are built right into the leading mobile operating systems like iOS and Android.

7

MOBILIZING
SOCIAL MEDIA

As we consider our mobile web context, we cannot deny the overwhelming influence and importance of social media. Fortunately, there are some quick and simple strategies to take advantage of when mobilizing your web site that extend beyond your site to a variety of social destinations.

MOBILE "COMES FREE" WITH MOST SOCIAL MEDIA

So are you ready for a short break from technical design and development? Great, I am too! Because this chapter dives into an area where a lot of the design and development is already done for us—we as mobile designers and developers merely need to leverage it in our mobilization effort.

This chapter also finally does what any decent book about web design and development needs to do: it delves into strategy that goes beyond your own web site. After all, the web is great precisely because it is a *web of interconnectedness*, right? That means we need to take a trip outside the confines of our own little corner of the web.

And what better place to do this than in the social realm? In addition to being technologically connected like the rest of the web, the social web is inherently connected at a more profound human level. Social networks have not taken off the way that they have because everyone just revels in the web technology behind them. It's actually for the opposite reason: when done well, the web technology is practically transparent.

So that's why we need to take a tour of the social web, to see where it is done well and can be leveraged for our own mobilization efforts. Because here's the big, juicy secret about the mobile social web: there's a great deal out there already that comes at no additional cost to us. It's free. We just have to link to it and let the already-mobilized social networks do the rest.

With that, let's buckle up and depart on a tour. First we'll inventory what we have to work with on the mobile web at large. Later in the chapter, we'll make a few tweaks to make sure that we've mobilized social as best as we can on our own site.

Our first stop is Twitter, my personal favorite hangout on the social web. And by the way, please bear with me: for permission reasons, I am using my own accounts and profiles as examples for this chapter (sorry if it unintentionally comes across as a bit narcissistic, but it was a lot easier to secure my own permission!).

I am starting with Twitter because I find Twitter's web application to be the best mobile social web experience in the list that we are checking out. Just compare the desktop version (**Figure 7.1**) to the mobile version (**Figure 7.2**).

First of all, the brand and UI design aesthetic are carried through from desktop to mobile very tastefully and consistently. But most importantly, Twitter's mobile web design is ideally suited for its use on the go. The sizing and legibility of everything is spot-on.

So with the first stop on our mobile social web tour, you learn that you can link directly to a Twitter profile from its corresponding mobile web site and you automatically get a free mobile version of Twitter. Nice! Fast!

And easy!

Next stop: Facebook.

FIGURE 7.1 (left) Twitter in the desktop version of Safari.

FIGURE 7.2 (right) Twitter in the mobile version of Safari.

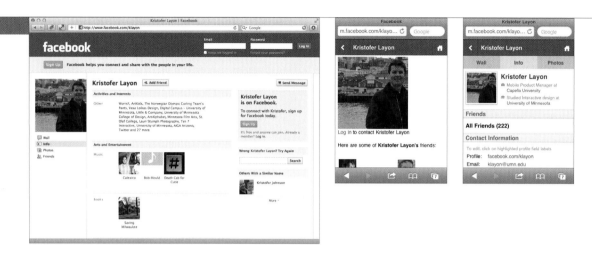

FIGURE 7.3 (left) Facebook in the desktop version of Safari.

FIGURE 7.4 (middle) Facebook in the mobile version of Safari.

FIGURE 7.5 (right) Facebook in the mobile version of Safari, after logging in.

Facebook ends up ranking quite high, too, for its mobile web presentation. Let's take a look (**Figurea 7.3**, **7.4**, and **7.5**).

Note that similar to Twitter, the experience is optimized to the mobile context quite well. The unauthenticated view (Figure 7.4), with the profile photo being really big, is not quite as well proportioned. But Facebook is also delivering less content in the public view, so perhaps this can be forgiven because Facebook does a very fine job of presenting an entire profile after logging in (Figure 7.5).

Once again, I cannot emphasize enough that this mobile presentation of your personal Facebook profile comes free. It's already there! All you need to do is link to it from your mobilized web site.

And we'll learn some tips for doing so after our assessment of the social web concludes. But without further delay, on to social web stop number three: Google+.

The newest social space on the block, Google+, comes out of the gates rather swiftly with its mobile optimization. Let's take a look. Here is how the full-screen presentation (**Figure 7.6**) compares to the mobilized version (**Figure 7.7**).

Google has a bit of a mixed blessing on its hands due to its many products—it is not just one single, focused tool like Twitter. Or even just a more multifaceted social tool like Facebook. Google is an entire cloud-based application platform of mail, chat, document, calendar, and many other online tools. The strength of this is that adding a more robust social channel to its established suite means that it has a large built-in audience of millions who will see and consider it from the beginning. And if this social channel integrates well with these other tools, it should go well for them.

(But at the time of this writing, all of this remains to be seen!)

The downside of this broad integration is that Google tries to make many of its tools visible at once, regardless of where you are. This is apparent in the mobile presentation of Google+, where about 20 percent of the visible screen is dominated by a navigation that goes to Gmail, Talk, Calendar, and other options in a dropdown menu. Will our divided attention be Google's strength or weakness in social?

Only time will tell—but as this plays out, at least we see that Google delivers a nicely-tailored mobile experience with good screen layout, navigation, and text and image scaling that is appropriate for mobile use. Another example of mobile out of the box, and free for us to use as long as we link to it!

FIGURE 7.6 (left) Google+ in the desktop version of Safari.

FIGURE 7.7 (right) Google+ in the mobile version of Safari.

QUORA

FIGURE 7.8 (left) Quora in the desktop version of Safari.

FIGURE 7.9 (right) Quora in the mobile version of Safari.

I will admit that despite having a Quora account, I do not participate in this social network very much. But when comparing their desktop (**Figure 7.8**) and mobile (**Figure 7.9**) presentations, I have to say that Quora has it nailed quite solidly.

The move to mobile on Quora feels very smooth and seamless. The text and image content is scaled very well and the Quora branding very consistently ties together the large and small screen experiences. There is also a nicely-emphasized call to action: the green Follow button is very prominent in the upper right corner. Followers, following, and mention counts are high in the information hierarchy.

So chalk up a win for Quora for their mobilized web presentation. It is well-done and designed to get you actively working right away, without any unnecessary pinching and zooming.

I consider LinkedIn to be the Facebook of the social business world, and I mean that in both good and bad ways. Bad in that it is not as tightly focused as a platform like Twitter, but good in that its presentation of connections helps get you connected. And its integration with other social networks has improved over time. Overall, it's a very solid and popular platform. So how does its full-screen (**Figure 7.10**) experience compare to its mobile (**Figure 7.11**) experience?

Ouch, LinkedIn! That hurts! LinkedIn does not do any web mobilization to help us use LinkedIn on small screens. Despite having some native mobile apps (iPhone, Blackberry, Android, and Palm at the time of this writing), there is no mobile-optimized presentation of our public profiles on the web.

Interestingly, LinkedIn does offer a middle ground: it has a touch-enabled mobile web application called LinkedIn Mobile available at http://touch.www.linkedin.com (**Figure 7.12**).

As my screenshot illustrates, it's a well-designed mobile web application, so I'll grant them that win. However, it is odd that LinkedIn chose to not stretch their mobile effort to public views of their web site as the previous social networks have done. LinkedIn has native and mobile web *applications* covered thoroughly; but for social web optimization that is available outside authentication, LinkedIn leaves us with pinching and zooming.

FIGURE 7.10 (left) LinkedIn in the desktop version of Safari.

FIGURE 7.11 (middle) LinkedIn in the mobile version of Safari.

FIGURE 7.12 (right) LinkedIn's mobile web app at http://touch.www.linkedin.com. It's nice, but it requires an account and authentication to see anything mobile-optimized.

FIGURE 7.13 (left) YouTube in the desktop version of Safari.

FIGURE 7.14 (right) YouTube in the mobile version of Safari.

Last but not least, let's take a look at YouTube—it's easy to forget that social platforms and rich media platforms are merging more and more. So as you mobilize your web site, you may want to consider integrating with any of your rich media platforms that have mature social components. YouTube is a prime example, given its integration with other Google platforms. And as we check out YouTube in the desktop (**Figure 7.13**) and mobile (**Figure 7.14**), this is what we see.

And we end this tour on a high note: YouTube is another platform that provides a great mobile-optimized presentation for free!

So after checking out these six social destinations, do not let your own mobile social investigations end here. Consider rich media, geolocation, and other web applications with social platforms that you participate in when mobilizing your web projects. Take advantage of any free mobile optimization that you can leverage. And if a favorite service doesn't yet deliver a decent mobile experience, let them know.

You might just be the tipping point for prioritizing a mobile optimized experience in someone's user story backlog!

CONNECTING TO SOCIAL

Now that we've identified a few choice mobile-optimized web properties to connect to from our own, how should we do it?

The first step is to build a small new block of social code, such as the Twitter link that I had in my page layout (refer to Figure 2.4 in Chapter 2), in a div that is being hidden in the mobile presentation. So here are a few short lines of code that I am placing at the end of the page, after the content and above the footer:

```
<div class="span-24 last" id="social">
<ul>
<li class="topline"><a href="http://www.twitter.com/
 klayon">Twitter</a>
   </li>
<li><a href="http://www.facebook.com/klayon">Facebook</a></li>
<li><a href="http://www.youtube.com/layonfamily">YouTube</a></li>
</ul>
</div>
```

As you can see, I am now changing my web strategy a bit due to what I have just learned about mobile presentations across social platforms. I'm not just linking to Twitter anymore; as long as Facebook and YouTube have such nice mobile optimizations, why not link to them, too?

But for expediency's sake, let's say that I don't want to redesign this into my regular full browser implementation (because I don't, which I know might be kind of silly—but this isn't about optimizing my desktop presentation). So I'm not going to display this new social block in my desktop version of the site, and will hide it instead with main.css:

```
#social {display: none;}
```

Next is the styling of the mobile presentation. It is a lot like the styling of my main mobile navigation, but I have elected to make the rows a bit shorter, use a blue background color, and not employ a gradient:

```
#social {
    display: inline;
}
#social ul {
    position: static;
    list-style-type: none;
    line-height: 36px;
    overflow: hidden;
```

```
        float: none;
        width: 100%;
        padding: 0;
        margin-top: 30px;
        margin-right: 0;
        margin-bottom: 0;
        margin-left: 0;
}
#social li {
        display: inline;
        width: 100%;
        margin: 0;
        font-size: 12pt;
}
#social a {
        display: block;
        font-weight: bold;
        line-height: 2em;
        width: auto;
        float: none;
        margin: 0;
        padding-top: 0;
        padding-right: 20px;
        padding-bottom: 0;
        padding-left: 20px;
        border-bottom-width: 1px;
        border-bottom-style: solid;
        border-bottom-color: #666;
        background-color: #CEEAFF;
}
```

FIGURE 7.15 The new social links in the mobile presentation of *Design in Finland*.

```
#social a:hover, #social a:focus {
    text-decoration: none;
    padding-top: 0;
    padding-right: 20px;
    padding-bottom: 0;
    padding-left: 20px;
    border-bottom-width: 1px;
    border-bottom-style: solid;
    border-bottom-color: #666;
}
```

What are the results? Let's take a look (**Figure 7.15**).

So once again, with almost no change to our existing site's markup or CSS files, I was able to add a small new social code block in the site's page template and style it in the new mobile.css stylesheet that kicks it into action on small screens.

Another example of iterative mobilization, without having to start over!

WRAPPING **UP**

In this chapter, you took a bit of a break from HTML and CSS development and focused on a mobile inventory of social networks and services. You learned that several mobile services provide out-of-the-box social mobilization for free!

All you need to do is provide a nice set of mobile-optimized links to drive your site visitors to these social media services, and their device detection does the rest of the work for you. Consequently, connecting your mobile presentation to these social web sites results in an ever-expanding, mobile-optimized World Wide Web that you are actively contributing to with your new mobile design chops.

And it doesn't even require a complete redesign of your existing site!

8

MOBILIZING
CONTENT STRATEGY

Content strategy is both the end of a
process and the beginning of another.
It is where getting familiar with mobile presentation options and
iteratively improving a legacy web site leads you to start question-
ing the very essence of what you are trying to optimize.

And the essence is the content.

UNDERSTANDING MOBILE CONTEXT FIRST LEADS TO A BETTER CONTENT STRATEGY

In this chapter, we start concluding the narrative arc of this book. The book began with exploring the big-picture mobilization effort of changing the entire user experience of a web site and then proceeded to explore how all of the elements of a typical site could be optimized for improved mobile presentation: layout, navigation, images, text, and forms.

And we even did a quick survey of social media sites to see where we can get some extra mobile bang for no additional mobile bucks.

Now we come full circle. We need to realize that we have become as familiar as we can with the mechanics of mobile presentation and optimization. We have mastered tweaks to our HTML markup and learned new ways to responsively position and style content in our CSS files. We have learned how to move our content, make it bigger or smaller, or even just hide it and get some of it out of the way.

So finally, we need to come face to face with reality: to make additional progress forward, we need to revisit the content itself.

Yes, I know — up until now, I have gone with the assumption that the content is king. That it has already been written, vetted, edited, polished, and aged so that it emits a gentle glow of meaningful perfection. I have gone with the assumption that the content simply needed only a mobile makeover.

But I know better. It probably needs more than that.

MOBILIZED DESIGN PREPARES
YOU FOR USABILITY EVALUATION

FIGURE 8.1 Mobile presentation of web content is like packing carry-on luggage: until you have the actual suitcase, how do you decide what to pack (and how much)?

After learning the ins and outs of mobile-optimized presentation, it is probably time to consider a more complete evaluation of what you are trying to optimize in the first place: the words and the images that comprise the content of the site.

But please don't see this as an avoidance measure. We did not start with user experience, layout, navigation, and so on merely to avoid dealing with improving content. This isn't like college where we partied all weekend doing the fun design, and we have to buckle down and focus on the real work now that we've made it to Sunday night.

Rather, learning responsive approaches to good mobile presentation helps us to see our content in a new context. It allows us to take these initial results of our mobilization efforts and ask our bosses and visitors for feedback.

Another way to look at this is that it's kind of like packing everything into a carry-on to bring on a flight so that you don't need to check any luggage, right? You do not really know how much you can bring and how to scale your range of needs across the small volume that you have, until you know the size of that space and can see how your things fit into the limitations of that carry-on luggage (**Figure 8.1**).

So now that you have learned how to design a mobile version of your site, you can actually see how your web belongings fit into a mobile context.

Now it's time to start prioritizing those belongings and pack accordingly!

I can't tell you how much I've learned about design and content strategy in the usability lab. As I always tell my clients, "This design is not necessarily the best solution. It is merely our best guess given what we know." Similarly, the content in a web site is usually also a best guess. Someone smart may have written it and someone smart no doubt edited it.

But as with design, the proof is in the visitor's use and interpretation. Does our design really get them to do what we want and does our content really tell them what we want them to hear?

So taking the analogy of packing the carry-on luggage a bit further, the task that we have at hand isn't just packing the right amount (and mix) of things for a different context. Perhaps that can be challenging enough.

The real challenge is that we're not packing for ourselves. *We're packing someone else's stuff.*

Now how is that going to go if we just sneak off on our own and do it by ourselves?

Probably not very well!

That is why, in my opinion, usability evaluation and content strategy are complementary. They always have been and always will be. I know this because I have learned two categories of information whenever I have gone into a usability evaluation for a web site.

WHAT THE SITE SAYS

Although, as a designer, I head into usability evaluations excited to learn whether my design is effective and attractive to someone who is using the site, much of the feedback is about words. The feedback is rarely, if ever, about things like "I'm seeing this header and think it is gorgeous—what is the typeface used there?" or "This multi-column layout is so elegant and useful!"

Rather, the feedback is usually about issues such as "I'm reading this page and do not really understand what it is saying," or "I'm looking for X and can't find it."

And the thing is, the X they are looking for is usually there. Sometimes it is staring them right in the face. But it may be called something slightly different than what they're seeking or concealed in a lengthy exposition that rambles on about everything related to X.

HOW THE SITE IS ORGANIZED

And that leads to the other large category of lessons learned in most web usability evaluations. After learning a lot about what a client's site does and does not say to visitors, we tend to get a lot of feedback and suggestions on organizational details. This can include critiques of the navigation (such as the number and names of categories), how information is grouped by section or page, and how information is organized or "chunked" into portions and distributed across a layout or multiple pages.

So in my opinion, the best beginning to a solid content strategy (and, in this particular case, a mobile content strategy) is to have it begin with your usability evaluation. Do not attempt to inventory, review, and rework any of your content in a silo or up on a mountaintop. Doing so is incredibly risky—as risky as it would be to pack that carry-on luggage for someone else without asking them anything about what you are packing for them!

CONTENT STRATEGY PREPARES YOU FOR MOBILE FIRST DESIGN

So hopefully you can see how these steps interlock into a good mobile workflow. By implementing some incremental techniques on your presentation layer, you can mobilize the content that you already have and then cue it up for usability evaluation. And learn a lot.

But the other thing is, you have probably learned more than just content feedback and criticism. And even if some of the critiques or suggestions sound like they involve content, they may instead involve aspects of design. Remember, it is all intertwined. A great mobile user experience is not just good content and okay design, nor is it good design but merely adequate content.

A great user experience is great content … that is also designed great!

MOVING FROM MOBILE LATER TO MOBILE FIRST?

By placing your usability evaluation after some initial mobilization steps of a legacy web site, you can be better prepared to make a bigger decision: have you learned enough about mobile design optimization and mobile content optimization to proceed to a new mobile first design?

Now please realize, I describe these steps as if they just happened in the span of a few days, and that's actually not what I mean. You should realize that the steps of incremental mobile improvement, just on the presentation layer alone, could roll out over a period of days, weeks, or even months. I'm not necessarily encouraging you to just jump in and sprint through this book's techniques as fast as you can. You might be able to, but your site may be more complex than the examples illustrated here or you may need to make more slow and iterative changes to your site over a period of time for other business reasons.

But that can be okay. It can still be a lot easier to do some incremental mobile optimization in the background than it is to ask for a big redesign budget for a new mobile site, right?

THEN INVENTORY AND STRATEGIZE CONTENT FIRST, TOO

If you ever do move from a more iterative, incremental mobilization effort to a full mobile first redesign that rethinks your web site for mobile from the beginning of the design process, be sure to create the time and expectations for a full inventory of your site content. Use what you learn during usability evaluation or just from everyday user feedback to prompt you to first rethink (and possibly rewrite!) your content, your information architecture, and your overall strategy for getting content to people. Is it just via the web site itself or do you need to revisit your social strategy as well? And what does all of this mean for long-term maintenance?

WRAPPING UP

This chapter discussed how the process of iterative, incremental, responsive mobile design should then lead to usability evaluation. Usability evaluation can then be the first step towards reevaluating your content and content strategy. And as you make this commitment, it can also create an opportunity to continue evaluating your mobile presentation strategy: is it time to step further ahead with a new mobile first design?

PROJECT INTERVIEW 3

INTERCONTINENTAL
HOTEL GROUP

In my experience, mobile users expect to get your content anytime from any smart device. They have incredibly high expectations—expectations set by some very well-designed mobile apps and sites that are, in some cases, superior in design and experience to their desktop counterparts.

But this means that your content has to work harder than ever. And that means your plans to mobilize your website can't leave out some careful attention paid to your content.

FIGURE PI 3.1 (left) Holiday Inn search results in a desktop browser.

FIGURE PI 3.2 (right) Holiday Inn search results in a mobile browser.

I know what you're thinking. "Can't I just tell people to cut the content for mobile and be done with it?" No! If you—or someone on your team—doesn't plan properly for content, you risk

- Including too much or too little content.

- Creating design templates that don't fit the content.

- Making content difficult to access, use, read, or understand.

- Making content more complicated to manage.

To help you plan, I chatted with Colleen Jones, author of *Clout: The Art and Science of Influential Web Content*, to ask her about mobile content strategy. Colleen was incredibly kind to take some time out of her writing and consulting schedule to answer these questions. Thanks, Colleen!

WHERE SHOULD PEOPLE START WITH MOBILIZING CONTENT?

Take an inventory of the content on your website using a tool such as SiteOrbiter. Then review a sample of it yourself. Get a feel for how current and appropriate it is for your users' mobile tasks. If you find a product description from 1998, for example, be afraid.

Honestly, you will probably find the content is a mess. Take heart in that you're not alone. The temptation is to shovel that mess of content into a mobile version of the site or into a mobile application. Don't do it! Resist! Instead, use your mobilizing effort as an opportunity to point out any of your website's content problems—so you can get help with solving them for both the website and its mobile version.

SHOULD PEOPLE MOBILIZE ALL OF THEIR CONTENT? WHY OR WHY NOT?

Yes and no. I love this question because it's actually a trick question. You can't possibly answer it without understanding

- How much content you have.

- Whether that content supports the most important or common tasks your users will do on mobile.

- Where your content is (in a CMS, etc.).

There is no definitive right or wrong answer here. If anyone tells you to mobilize all, some, or none of your content without understanding your situation first, run far, far away.

Is your website very large or for a very large company? Then I recommend making your effort to mobilize content start small, then grow. Begin with a pilot, make it successful, then expand that pilot with more mobilized content. For example, InterContinental Hotel Group (IHG) created a very simple mobile version of Holiday Inn. The content simply included a few details about the property and the room, and that was enough for their customers to start using it to book a trip. Since then, IHG has mobilized sites for their other brands.

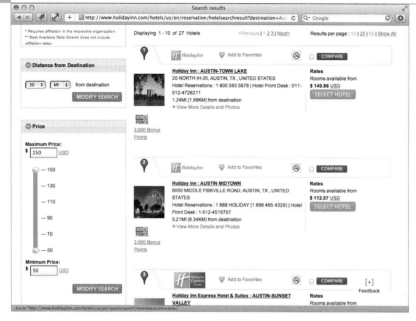

FIGURE PI 3.3 (left) Holiday Inn hotel details in a desktop browser.

FIGURE PI 3.4 (right) Holiday Inn hotel details in a mobile browser.

HOW DOES CONTENT NEED TO BE ADJUSTED FOR MOBILE?

As you might guess, this also depends. Sometimes the mobile version of a site should have alternative versions of content, such as

- Shorter titles

- Shorter descriptions, callouts, etc.

- Smaller images or images that can dynamically scale in size

- Fewer images

Let's go back to the Holiday Inn example. Photos help booking. Most people want to look at photos of a particular Holiday Inn hotel before they book it. On the website, each Holiday Inn hotel can have around 20 photos. That's fine if you're browsing from a desktop or laptop. But, that doesn't work so well for a mobile phone. If you're trying to book a hotel in a rush and with a small screen, you don't need to browse 20 photos. In fact, that many photos can be a hindrance. So, IHG is figuring out how to use only the most appropriate photos for the mobilized site.

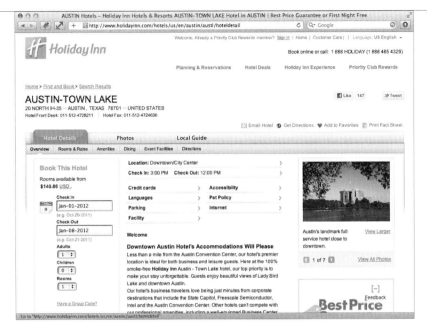

The catch here is you do NOT necessarily want to create an entirely separate mobile version of all of your content. That would take a long time, and could be a nightmare to manage. Instead, you want to re-use as much content as possible and optimize, where necessary, for mobile (this is where responsive design can help win the day). It's also where a good content management system can come in handy.

HOW CAN A CONTENT MANAGEMENT SYSTEM HELP PEOPLE MOBILIZE CONTENT?

A content management system, used well, can reuse your web content for mobile. Some systems can also help you collect alternative versions of content, such as shorter titles, for the mobile version.

If you already have a content management system, you might find changes are in order. For example, you might need to add fields to the pages where your writers/editors/content creators post content. You might, for instance, need to add a field that collects a shorter version of the web page title. Or, you might need to add a way to flag different sizes of photos to work for different mobile experiences.

FIGURE PI 3.5 (left) Holiday Inn detailed results and photos in a desktop browser.

FIGURE PI 3.6 (right) Holiday Inn detailed results and photos in a mobile browser.

DOES CHANGING CONTENT FOR MOBILE CHANGE
HOW PEOPLE WRITE OR EDIT CONTENT?

No and yes. Another trick question! The answer is no in that best practices for web writing tend to work for mobile writing. For example, chunking content is critical to making it work well across your web and mobile sites.

I would add a best practice: avoid referencing the screen layout or format (for example, Look at the image on the right.) Why? Because the design of a screen will vary depending on whether a user views it from a computer or a mobile device. You cannot write as if you know the user's display.

While the best practices largely hold up, something about writing for mobile does change. Process. Creating content for your main website and a mobile version without losing your mind means you have to plan writing and editing for both. Many writers and editors have to get used to writing for both, such as writing alternative versions of descriptions and gathering alternative versions of photos. You also need the right tools to guide the process. For example, I helped CDC create a tool kit to guide communicators in writing content for mobile. I included guidelines, tips, and plenty of examples.

So, as you mobilize your website, remember to mobilize your content. I guarantee you'll have less hassle, fewer unwelcome surprises, and much happier users.

9

OTHER WAYS TO MOBILIZE: JQUERY MOBILE

Besides custom designing your own
mobile presentation of web content,
there are several mobile frameworks that are available. These
touch-optimized web frameworks provide some wonderful design
patterns and efficiencies for your projects. One mobile framework
that has been in development for over a year and is becoming
well-established is jQuery Mobile. Because so many web designers and developers are already familiar with jQuery, I thought it
would be useful to demonstrate how to apply jQuery Mobile to
our Design in Finland case study.

THE **JQUERY MOBILE** WEB **FRAMEWORK**

FIGURE 9.1
The jQuery Mobile web site
(http://jquerymobile.com/).

FIGURE 9.1
The jQuery Mobile web site
(http://jquerymobile.com/).

I really enjoy designing custom navigations and themes for many of my web projects, but there are also times when I prefer the approach of using an existing framework to solve some of my project design needs.

In fact, the Design in Finland responsive case study uses the Blueprint CSS framework for the grid layout and typography in its full-screen version. I could certainly design my own CSS framework—but I don't find the Blueprint framework to be particularly limiting and using it allows me to more quickly move on to the detailed design problems that I like to spend my time on.

Now that I have explored, in a more nuanced way, how to mobilize an existing web site by focusing on user experience, layout, navigation, and content, I would like to turn our attention to a more app-like web framework that solves mobile presentation differently: jQuery Mobile (**Figure 9.1**).

ADVANTAGES AND DISADVANTAGES OF JQUERY MOBILE

jQuery Mobile is a lightweight, mobile-optimized framework that is built on top of the popular jQuery JavaScript framework. Some advantages of using jQuery Mobile include:

- Spending less time designing and coding.

- Incorporating predesigned layout, control, and widget elements.

- Bringing attractive transitions and effects to your mobile site that are normally only expected in native mobile apps (e.g., iOS and Android).

- Being confident that your mobile site will gracefully adapt to a large variety of mobile devices.

So are there any disadvantages to using jQuery Mobile? Sure, there are a few to consider:

- Replacing some of your HTML with new markup that is required for jQuery Mobile to influence your site's appearance and behavior.

- Taking time to learn someone else's CSS and JavaScript framework instead of spending the time to write your own.

- Applying jQuery Mobile to multiple web projects could make them look more similar than you prefer.

- Using jQuery Mobile in a responsive manner could be quite challenging, if not impossible, so you should only use it where you are comfortable redirecting people to a separate mobile site (or where you are comfortable with the jQuery Mobile presentation also being your desktop presentation—this is certainly becoming more common).

Now that you know the pluses and minuses of using jQuery Mobile, let's take a look and see how we can apply it to our Design in Finland case study. I will start with the home page and work my way through the HTML section by section.

HEAD

Taking a look at the page's head section first, here is the HTML, with the new elements required for jQuery Mobile highlighted:

```
<head>
<meta charset="utf-8">
<meta name="viewport" content="width=device-width, initial-scale=1">
<title>Design in Finland</title>
<link rel="shortcut icon" href="images/favicon.ico"
    type="image/x-icon" />
<link rel="stylesheet" href="http://code.jquery.com/mobile/latest/
jquery.mobile.min.css" rel="stylesheet" type="text/css" />
<link href="css/main.css" rel="stylesheet" type="text/css">
<link href="css/mobile.css" rel="stylesheet" media="screen and
(max-width: 768px)" type="text/css" />
<script src="http://code.jquery.com/jquery-1.6.4.min.js"></script>
<script src="http://code.jquery.com/mobile/latest/
jquery.mobile.min.js"></script>
</head>
```

These three new lines of code can be broken down into two essential components. The first component, a new stylesheet, is specific to jQuery Mobile and contains all of the layout and style parameters for this mobile web framework. The second component enables all of the jQuery Mobile behavior and features links to two JavaScript files.

Note that I have still retained the two stylesheets from our first case study, `main.css` and `mobile.css`. I will be making a few adjustments to them, but several of their rules will still apply to the jQuery Mobile version of the web site.

> **TIP:** In this example, the links to the stylesheet and JavaScript files go out to http://code.jquery.com. That's because I am taking advantage of the hosted files. It is much faster and easier than downloading and setting it up on your own server!
>
> For more information about downloading jQuery Mobile or using the free hosted option, visit: http://jquerymobile.com/download/.

So this first step is not very hard and makes a lot of sense because it mirrors what we do whenever we adopt an existing web framework: we start with linking in to the framework's appearance and behaviors.

Next step: we start to pull the framework's HTML into the content area of the site's page template.

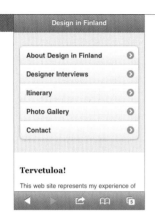

FIGURE 9.2 The Design in Finland index screen with jQuery Mobile's "Swatch B" applied.

Here is the index page's HTML as it continues beyond the head portion of the markup, with the new jQuery Mobile code highlighted:

```
<body>
<div data-role="page">
<div data-role="header" data-theme="b">
    <h1>Design in Finland</h1>
</div>
...
</div>
</body>
```

The two new `div`s, page and header, do exactly what they suggest: these elements use the data attributes of HTML5 to magically work with jQuery's JavaScript framework to provide a way for it to apply behaviors and themes to the mobile site's pages and header bars.

Next, a detail is specified in the second div: `data-theme="b"`. This specification gives our page some really nice mileage in the styling department. As jQuery Mobile's Theming Pages section (http://bit.ly/qVOeh6) explains, there are five predesigned themes to choose from. I found Swatch B's light blue theme particularly suitable for this site screen's header bar. So after setting the theme to b, this is the appearance of the new index page as styled by jQuery Mobile framework (**Figure 9.2**).

Looking good!

And now we can see what's coming next: adding some nice app-like style and behavior to the navigation.

jQuery Mobile really excels at providing graceful site navigation with many of the style and behavior details we have been conditioned by native iOS and Android apps to expect. But with jQuery Mobile, thanks to the growing power of CSS3, we can deploy a high-end mobile user experience to mobile web sites that is comparable to those native apps.

Let's take a look at the HTML behind this magic:

```
<div data-role="content">
<ul data-role="listview" data-inset="true">
    <li><a href="about.html">About Design in Finland</a></li>
    <li><a href="interviews.html">Designer Interviews</a></li>
    <li><a href="map.html">Itinerary</a></li>
    <li><a href="photos.html">Photo Gallery</a></li>
    <li><a href="contact.html">Contact</a></li>
</ul>
</div>
```

FIGURE 9.3 When About Design in Finland is tapped, there is a blue touch effect and an animated loading confirmation that briefly overlays the screen.

So the navigation is the same unordered list that I had in the site's original HTML. But it's been wrapped in a new div with the jQuery Mobile data-role set to content.

And what does this magic entail, you might ask? To begin with, there are some handsome touch effects for the buttons in this navigation as well as a helpful modal overlay message that tells you that the browser is loading a new screen (**Figure 9.3**).

But the jQuery Mobile wizardry continues to reveal itself! Next, there is the native app behavior of an animated screen transition. It's a nicely done CSS3 slide effect from right to left captured here (**Figure 9.4**) after several attempts at catching it at just the right moment. You're welcome!

So now we have arrived at the second screen of our new jQuery Mobilized web site where more great surprises await.

FIGURE 9.4 The screen slides from right to left as the browser transitions from Home to the About Design in Finland.

FIGURE 9.5 The About Design in Finland screen. The header bar is now a tool bar, too.

Now that we've arrived at an interior screen of our mobile web site, we can see that there are some differences from the home page. First, there are two new buttons in the header bar—so now it's a header tool bar (**Figure 9.5**).

jQuery Mobile provides some nice tool bar and button options right out of the box. How is this done? Once again, it's really just a matter of plugging in the right specifications into your new HTML template. The modifications are relatively minor:

```
<div data-role="header" data-position="inline" data-theme="b">
    <a href="index.html" data-icon="home" data-iconpos="notext"
        data-direction="reverse">Home</a>
            <h1>About</h1>
    <a href="menu.html" data-rel="dialog" data-transition=
        "slideup">Menu</a>
</div>
```

Now I realize that I highlighted nearly all of the new stuff here because this code block is mostly jQuery Mobile stuff. But it's still pretty straightforward, so let's take it one element at a time:

1. First, the h1 header About is wrapped in a new div. In the div, the role of header is specified—this styles the header bar. The inline specification instructs jQuery mobile to position any toolbar buttons horizontally inline. And the theme calls up the light blue theme that was applied to the home screen.

2. Next, a button is specified before the About header label. The link code creates this button automatically. Plus the specification of data-icon="home" pulls in a nice home icon. Finally, the data-iconpos="notext" specifies to not display the Home text (which is still required to be in the code). Last, the specification of data-direction="reverse" instructs this button to animate back to the home screen in the reverse direction (that is, left to right).

3. Finally, a second button is specified after the About header label. The link code does this automatically again. Next, the specification of data-rel= "dialog" instructs jQuery Mobile to transition the target screen of this link onto the page as a modal dialog (explained in the next section). Finally, the data-transition="slideup" specifies this modal screen to animate in by sliding up.

And it's the third part of this, the Menu button, that reinforces the second main change to the secondary screens of this jQuery Mobile site: I have elected to be more app-like in this design and only display the navigation on the home screen. In the rest of the site, I wanted the site to be more like a mobile app. The Menu buttons make this happen very nicely.

But how does it look (and work)? Let's see!

MODAL DIALOG MENU

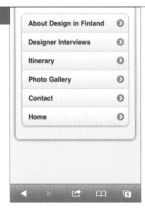

FIGURE 9.6 The new Design in Finland modal dialog Menu screen.

This screen might be my favorite part of this implementation of the jQuery Mobile framework: I really like how this web framework handles modal dialogs. Here is what it looks like when we pull the site's menu into a modal dialog screen (**Figure 9.6**).

Nice, huh?

Let's take a look under the hood to see how it works:

```
<div data-role="page" data-theme="e">

<div data-role="content">

    <ul data-role="listview" data-inset="true">

        <li><a href="about.html" data-transition=
            "slidedown">About Design in Finland</a></li>

        <li><a href="interviews.html" data-transition=
            "slidedown">Designer Interviews</a></li>

        <li><a href="map.html" data-transition=
            "slidedown">Itinerary</a></li>

        <li><a href="photos.html" data-transition=
            "slidedown">Photo Gallery</a></li>

        <li><a href="contact.html" data-transition=
            "slidedown">Contact</a></li>

        <li><a href="index.html" data-transition=
            "slidedown">Home</a></li>

    </ul>

</div>

</div>
```

NOTE: Note that the themes and transitions of jQuery Mobile require us to place styling parameters in our HTML, which does not adhere to clean separations between content, style, and behavior per best practices in web standards. *sigh*

Some of the HTML elements will look familiar to you. In fact, if you compare this code block to what is in the Navigation section of this chapter, there are two differences.

The first difference is that at the page level, I wanted this menu to be visually different so I chose a different jQuery Mobile theme (theme e, or yellow). I really like the brightness of this option. Here are the jQuery Mobile themes that you have to choose from:

- default (black and gray)
- theme a (all black)
- theme b (blue on gray)
- theme c (all gray)
- theme d (gray on white)
- theme e (all yellow)

The second difference from the home screen's navigation is the addition of `data-transition="slidedown"` to the li's (list items). This merely instructs the modal dialog screen to slide back down each time you navigate to a new page. I thought this transition was most appropriate given that the modal dialog slides up when it appears. But jQuery Mobile lets you customize transitions wherever you want with the `data-transition` property, so you have quite a bit of flexibility. Here are the transition options:

- slide (right to left)
- reverse (left to right)
- slideup
- slidedown
- pop
- fade
- flip

NOTE: According to the jQuery Mobile web site, flip is not yet well-supported on all Android devices because that platform does not consistently support CSS 3D transforms.

FIGURE 9.7 The jQuery Mobile version of the Design in Finland Contact form.

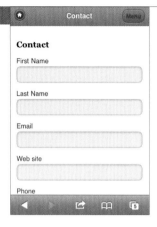

The last two sections of this chapter are pretty short and sweet. Short because there is no additional work required to implement jQuery Mobile and sweet because the results are elegant.

So here is the great news regarding the site's web form: porting over the contact form from the original version to the jQuery Mobile version did not require any additional changes! That is, no changes in the form code itself—just the same div data-role="page" after the body tag, and the same header bar code that is on every other page.

And here are the elegant results (**Figure 9.7**). jQuery Mobile delivers a nice form, does it not?

If you have a more complicated form, just visit jQuery Mobile's gallery of form controls (http://bit.ly/rv3xzZ) to see how different form elements will be handled.

FIGURE 9.8 The jQuery Mobile version of the Design in Finland in landscape orientation.

I did not want to wrap up this chapter without verifying how nicely jQuery Mobile handles landscape orientation (**Figure 9.8**).

Everything scales very well. And also note how, in this particular example, the mobile stylesheet from the previous mobile implementation still kicks in to change the dynamic photo grid layout from one column in portrait to two columns in landscape. Nice!

WRAPPING UP

In this chapter, you explored a second technique for quickly mobilizing an existing web site. The jQuery Mobile web framework is a really slick system to implement. It includes a complete CSS and JavaScript solution for native app-like appearance and behavior and requires minimal HTML modifications to make it all work. So if you prefer this method of working, these styles of screen transitions, and user experiences that are more comparable to a mobile app, use this chapter as your entry into the world of jQuery Mobile. And be sure to check out the jQuery Mobile web site to learn more than was demonstrated in this introduction to the framework.

Finally, to download the complete jQuery Mobile version of the Design in Finland web site demonstrated in this chapter, visit http://www.mobilizingwebsites.net/jquery/jqmdownload.zip.

10

OTHER WAYS TO MOBILIZE: **DEVICE DETECTION** AND **PHP INCLUDES**

As we wrap up this book's survey of different approaches to mobilizing web sites, we conclude with a third method to consider. Rather than querying the screen size of a display's viewport to determine how to present content, this approach instead detects hardware type. And instead of serving a fixed HTML page and responsively presenting that page with different CSS rules for mobile contexts, you will learn how to have your web server dynamically construct and serve a different page based on the device on which it will appear.

WHAT IS PHP?

PHP is a server-side scripting language, as opposed to HTML which is a markup language that can be interpreted directly on the client-side of a web interaction. PHP is a little newer than HTML, but not by much. Tim Berners-Lee released the first public version of HTML in 1991. Then in 1994, another fellow by the name of Rasmus Lerdorf started writing some small programs (or scripts) that helped him maintain his web site—and he first called these Personal Home Page Tools. While its acronym was first derived from Rasmus's initial work, subsequent development by others has pushed the meaning of PHP to now stand for PHP Hypertext Pre-processor (and here I learned something new: this is called a *recursive acronym*).

NOTE: For more information about PHP, visit http://en.wikipedia.org/wiki/HTML and http://www.php.net/manual/en/history.php.php.

So in practice, PHP and HTML are quite different—but they can also be used in tandem to do some pretty cool things. If PHP is new to you, think of it as using JavaScript to enhance the behavior of your HTML by either embedding it in your HTML or linking to a separate file with a .js file extension. In this case, we will do something similar: embed some of the PHP right in our HTML and also refer to external PHP files that will have .php file extensions.

While the differences in how JavaScript and PHP work are more or less transparent to people who use web sites, the key difference for us is that PHP only functions on web servers that run a PHP processor. When encountering PHP inside HTML, the PHP processor dynamically processes the PHP commands. These PHP commands can output HTML or sometimes pull in—or *include*—additional PHP or HTML files. We call such snippets *PHP includes*.

So let's take a look at how PHP can be used to mobilize a web site.

ENABLING PHP ON WEB SERVERS

PHP processing is almost always a standard service option in web hosting packages, so you should not have to pay anything extra for this functionality. If you have any questions, you should contact a customer service representative (or check out the account options) for your hosting company.

Beyond verifying that you have PHP processing as an option, you will also need to verify whether it is enabled (sometimes you can do this yourself via a control panel, otherwise request that your service provider enable it for you). Finally, it's important to note which version of PHP is running on your web server. The current version is 5, but because of differences between versions, some web servers still only support version 4 or even earlier versions.

The PHP used in this case study runs on version 4 and newer.

If you want to verify that PHP can be processed on your server yourself, just create a file called test.php with the following contents:

```
<?php
phpinfo();
?>
```

If it is processed properly, a bunch of results will be returned, including the version of PHP on the server.

USING PHP

The good news is that PHP can be implemented with minimal changes to your existing HTML pages. The next sections will explore what can stay the same and what needs to change.

MODIFYING YOUR HTML FILES

The first thing you will do for this method is change your file extension from .html to .php. By doing this, your server's PHP processor will know that it needs to process these pages differently.

Next, let's take a look at what needs to change inside the markup that you already have. I'll use the home (index.php) page as the example:

```php
<?php include($_SERVER['DOCUMENT_ROOT'] . '/site2/' .
→  'includes/session.inc.php'); ?>

<!DOCTYPE html>

<html>

<head>

<meta http-equiv="Content-Type" content="text/html; charset=UTF-8" />

<title>Design in Finland</title>

<!-- Blueprint CSS Framework include -->

<link rel="shortcut icon" href="images/favicon.ico"
→  type="image/x-icon" />

<link href="css/blueprint/screen.css" rel="stylesheet"
→  type="text/css" media="screen" />

<link href="css/blueprint/print.css" rel="stylesheet"
→  type="text/css" media="print" />

<link href="css/main.css" rel="stylesheet" type="text/css"
→  media="screen" />

<link href="css/mobile.css" rel="stylesheet" media="screen and
→  (max-width: 768px)" type="text/css" />

<!--[if IE]>

<link rel="stylesheet" href="css/blueprint/ie.css" type="text/css"
→  media="screen, projection" />

<![endif]-->

<?php include($_SERVER['DOCUMENT_ROOT'] . '/site2/' .
→  'includes/head.inc.php'); ?>

</head>
```

These first two modifications tell the server to grab two include files, session. inc.php and head.inc.php, and dynamically insert them into the page. What these PHP includes do will be explained in the next section of this chapter.

Then the third modification to the HTML looks like this and it follows the content area of the markup:

```
<div class="span-24 last" id="footer">

<div id="footer_inner">

<ul class="copyright">

<li>Copyright &copy; 2011 <a href=http://www.aesthetesoftware.com/
⇥ target="_blank">Aesthete Software, LLC</a>.</li>

<li>All rights reserved.</li>

</ul>

</div>

</div>

<div class="span-24 last" id="fullsite">

<ul>

<li class="topline">

<?phpif(isset($_SESSION['full'])) {

    echo '<a id="return_mobile" href="javascript:mobile_site()">Return
    ⇥ to mobile site</a>';

}else if(isset($_SESSION['mobile'])) {

    echo '<a href="javascript:full_site()">View full site</a>';

}

?>

</li>

</ul>

</div>

</div>

</body>

</html>
```

FIGURE 10.1 (left) The View Full Site button in the mobile presentation.

FIGURE 10.2 (right) The Return to Mobile site button in the full site presentation.

It's this last HTML change that does something pretty cool with our PHP-powered mobile presentation alternative. It delivers an option where mobile visitors can opt out of the mobile presentation and see the full screen presentation (**Figure 10.1**).

And, if visitors to the site change their minds and want to return to the mobile-optimized presentation, they are presented with that option in the full screen version (**Figure 10.2**).

So to make this happen, the last modification to the HTML includes a few more lines of PHP right in the markup. It tells the pages to either display the **View full site** message in the mobile presentation or the **Return to mobile site** message in the full screen presentation. These choices are presented as buttons and allow visitors to toggle back and forth between the full site and mobilized presentation.

CSS STYLING FOR THE MOBILE AND FULL SCREEN BUTTONS

You'll notice that I decided to style the **View full site** and **Return to mobile site** buttons quite differently. The differences in style send a message that the mobile presentation is the new status quo on mobile devices. The **View full site** options blend into the design more, whereas the **Return to mobile site** button is styled very boldly. This bold design does not just make the **Return to mobile site** button easy to find, but suggests that the full screen view is something that can be turned off.

In other words, my styles are biased towards the mobile presentation and not the full site view. So if you implement this, be conscious of your design choices—you may wish to emphasize a slightly different message (or to a different degree) in your mobile presentation than what I have done here.

To see how my changes were done, let's first take a look at the styles for the **View full site** option in `mobile.css`. First, I added the #fullsite ID to the portion of the stylesheet that already resets several styles to be full width:

```
#banner, #nav, #secondarynav, #bodycontent, #rightbar, #footer,
 #social, #fullsite {
    width: 100%;
    margin: 0;
    padding: 0;
    border: none;
}
```

Next, I also added the `fullsite` ID to the rules that define the mobile social button presentation, as I wanted to piggyback off that look and make this look similar. So the modified rules are:

```
#social, #fullsite {...
#social ul, #fullsite ul {...
#social li, #fullsite li {...
#social a, #fullsite a {...
#social a:hover, #social a:focus, #fullsite a:hover, #fullsite
→ a:focus {...
```

Then I layered in some styling that is specific to the **View full site** option. This gives the button similar sizing and styling to make it coordinate with the social navigation above, but a different background color helps it stand out just a bit:

```
#fullsite a{
    background-color: #FFC;
    color: #003580;
}
```

That's it!

So what about how this area is styled in the full site view? To see how this was done, let's take a look at the styles for the **Return to mobile site** button in main.css:

```css
#fullsite {
    display: inline;
    margin: 0px;
    padding: 0px;
}
#fullsite ul {
    position: static;
    list-style-type: none;
    line-height: 48px;
    overflow: hidden;
    float: none;
    width: 100%;
    padding: 0;
    margin-top: 30px;
    margin-right: 0;
    margin-bottom: 30px;
    margin-left: 0;
}
#fullsite li {
    display: inline;
    width: 100%;
    margin: 0;
    font-size: 24pt;
    text-align: center;
}
```

```
#fullsite a {
    display: block;
    font-weight: bold;
    line-height: 2em;
    width: auto;
    float: none;
    margin: 0;
    padding: 0;
    background-color: #C00;
    color: #FFF;
}
#fullsite a:hover, #fullsite a:focus {
    text-decoration: none;
    padding: 0;
    border-bottom-width: 1px;
    border-bottom-style: solid;
    border-bottom-color: #666;
}
```

Note that this CSS looks quite similar to the mobile button styling I introduced in Chapter 3. That's because it is very similar—I wanted the button to be mobile-friendly, despite the rest of the full site view being in the typical desktop paradigm. On the other hand, I wanted to make sure that people see this button at the bottom of the full site layout on a small screen, so I beefed it up with a red background and a size that is scaled to mobile presentation.

Now that we see how these two options for toggling between presentations are styled, how do they work functionally?

ADDING PHP INCLUDES

Let's take a look at what one of these PHP includes looks like.
Here's session.inc.php:

```php
<?php$base_path = $_SERVER['DOCUMENT_ROOT'] . '/site2/';
require_once($base_path . 'includes/is_mobile_device.php');
```

```php
<?php $base_path = $_SERVER['DOCUMENT_ROOT'];
require_once($base_path . 'includes/is_mobile_device.php');

if (is_mobile_device()) {
    session_start();
    if($_GET['full'] == "1") {
        unset($_SESSION['mobile']);
        $_SESSION['full']=1;
    } else if($_GET['mobile'] == "1") {
        unset($_SESSION['full']);
        $_SESSION['mobile']=1;
    } else if(!isset($_SESSION['full'])) {
        $_SESSION['mobile'] = 1;
        unset($_SESSION['full']);
    }
}
?>
```

NOTE: Note that the line of code I highlighted includes /site2/ because these files are not running in the root directory of the server. Because you are probably using the root directory, you should omit /site2/ like so:

```php
<?php $base_path = $_SERVER['DOCUMENT_ROOT'];
require_once($base_path . 'includes/is_mobile_device.php');
```

So if you haven't programmed in PHP before, this probably looks a bit foreign to you. Though the section above isn't terribly different from JavaScript, having some familiarity with JavaScript can be helpful.

Basically, this file is governing the session state of the website. If the visitor is using a mobile device, a session state is set. This session state allows the website to remember whether the visitor wants to see the mobile or full version of the site. If the visitor switches views using the "View full site" or "Return to mobile site" links, the session state is updated accordingly.

DEVICE DETECTION

What about the device detection script, is_mobile_device.php? I am not going to reproduce the entire file here, as it is too long for that (you can get it as part of this chapter's download). But in a nutshell, the is_mobile_device.php file has the server reaching out to the visitor's device and detecting what type of device it is. It takes a first pass and looks for broader mobile platforms (iOS, Android, Symbian) and then goes through a much longer list of specific device types by type or network. So this section identifies everything from manufacturers like Nokia to carriers like T-Mobile.

> **NOTE:** Read more about how this works in the article "Lightweight Device-Detection in PHP" at http://mobiforge.com/developing/story/lightweight-device-detection-php.

The next file to take a look at is head_inc.php:

```php
<?php$base_path = $_SERVER['DOCUMENT_ROOT'] . '/site2/';
require_once($base_path . 'includes/is_mobile_device.php');

# Initilization Code
# -------------------
# Place path to full and mobile site head includes here
# Note: include leading and trailing backslashes

$full_site_loc = '/includes/full_site.inc.html';
$mobile_site_loc = '/includes/mobile.inc.html';

# End of Initialization Code
# Do not change anything below this line
# --------------------------------------

if (is_mobile_device() && isset($_SESSION['mobile'])) {
    include($base_path . $mobile_site_loc);
} else {
    include($base_path . $full_site_loc);
}
```

NOTE: Note that single-line comments in PHP are preceded by the # character. You can also wrap comments like you do in CSS (/* comment */).

This file defines the paths to the full and mobile site head PHP includes. In other words, after device detection takes place, this file instructs the server to insert one version of HTML (the mobile include) for the mobile presentation and another for the desktop, or full site, presentation (the full site include).

THE FULL SITE AND MOBILE PHP INCLUDES

Now that we have seen how device detection and mobile styling play a role, what is in these full site and mobile includes? First, here is full_site.inc.html:

```html
<!-- Blueprint CSS Framework include -->
<link rel="shortcut icon" href="../images/favicon.ico"
    type="image/x-icon" />
<link href="css/blueprint/screen.css" rel="stylesheet"
    type="text/css" media="screen" />
<link href="css/blueprint/print.css" rel="stylesheet"
    type="text/css" media="print" />
<link href="css/main.css" rel="stylesheet"
    type="text/css" media="screen" />
<!--[if IE]>
<link rel="stylesheet" href="css/blueprint/ie.css"
    type="text/css" media="screen, projection" />
<![endif]-->
<script type="text/javascript">
// Mobile site script
function mobile_site() {
    var url = window.location.href;
    url = url.split("?")[0];
    if(url.charAt(url.length-1) == "#") {
        url = url.slice(0,url.length-1);
    }
    url = url + "?mobile=1";
    window.location.replace(url);
}
</script>
```

And here is the mobile version:

```
<meta name="viewport" content="width=device-width,
→ initial-scale=1.0" />

<link href="css/mobile.css" rel="stylesheet" media="screen and
→ (max-width: 768px)" type="text/css" />

<script type="text/javascript">
// Full site script
function full_site() {
    var url = window.location.href;
    url = url.split("?")[0];
    if(url.charAt(url.length-1) == "#") {
        url = url.slice(0,url.length-1);
    }
    url = url + "?full=1";
    window.location.replace(url);
}
</script>
```

As the highlighted differences show, aside from the different stylesheet presentations, there is some dynamic URL naming going on as well. The JavaScript in each case denotes the full screen and mobile versions with different names, allowing the script in session.inc.php to update the session state and enable the mode switch to take place.

SOME DISTINGUISHING CSS

Last but not least, I thought it would be helpful to help distinguish this third mobile presentation from our other two mobile presentations, so I applied some different navigation styling. Here is the revised mobile.css:

```css
#nav ul {
    width: 100%;
    padding: 0;
    margin-top: 30px;
    margin-right: 0;
    margin-bottom: 0;
    margin-left: 0;}
#nav li {
    font-family: Georgia, "Times New Roman", Times, serif;
    width: 100%;
    margin: 0;
    font-size: 12pt;
    color: #333;
    font-weight: normal;
    text-align: center;
}
#nav a {
    line-height: 2.2em;
    width: auto;
    float: none;
    margin: 0;
    padding-top: 0;
    padding-bottom: 0;
    border-bottom-width: 1px;
```

FIGURE 10.3 The third mobile version of Design in Finland.

```
        border-bottom-style: solid;
        border-bottom-color: #666;
        background-color: #E3F3FF;
    }
    #nav a:hover, #nav a:focus {
        text-decoration: none;
        padding-top: 0;
        padding-bottom: 0;
        border-bottom-width: 1px;
        border-bottom-style: solid;
        border-bottom-color: #666;
    }
```

With these styles, the mobile navigation has a light blue background, slightly shorter buttons, and centered text that is set in the Georgia typeface (**Figure 10.3**).

This chapter has presented a third technique to consider for mobilizing a web site. By using PHP include files and a web server that runs PHP, you can present a web site that provides a way back to the full desktop experience from the mobile presentation.

And in the course of this demonstration, you also saw another way to style a mobile navigation!

To see the PHP-powered site demonstrated in this chapter, visit:
http://www.mobilizingwebsites.net/site2/

And to download all of the files, download:
http://www.mobilizingwebsites.net/site2.zip

CONCLUSION

The intention of this book was to lower the perceived bar for designing a mobile version of an existing web site. The very best approach to mobile redesign may be to start over completely, design both presentation and content for mobile devices first, then proceed to design for desktop browsers. But we know the realities of our schedules, budgets, and business constraints all too well to recognize that such an opportunity is not always available or preferable.

Plus, if you are unfamiliar or brand new to responsive design techniques, you may want to spend some additional time working with the techniques and how they can be applied to a site that you already understand before doing a more comprehensive mobile redesign.

So think of this book as a prequel, of sorts, to mobile first web design. I hope that the demonstrations on mobilizing screen layouts, site navigations and subnavigations, images, text, and forms encourage you to start designing mobile more quickly and with less concern. Just remember, baby steps are a great way to get started!

Of the three techniques demonstrated here, which one is right for you? That depends on a lot of factors like the site, its size and content, and your user experience expectations. Some distinguishing characteristics to remember:

- Custom mobile stylesheets with media queries (Chapters 2 through 8): This is the best way to learn how design for mobile works. It can also be tailored best to a site's brand. Finally, it leverages responsive design so you can work with just one set of source code without needing to branch to a separate mobile site.

- jQuery Mobile (Chapter 9): This method can result in behavior that feels more like a native mobile app. It comes out of the box with some nice design patterns and themes that result in a consistent user experience from screen to screen and across other details like buttons and form elements. But it does not use responsive design, so it is best-suited for a separate mobile experience that users get to via a mobile link or redirect from the main site.

- Device detection and PHP (Chapter 10): This technique is similar to the first technique in terms of style and behavior, so the results can be whatever you dream up. One advantage of using device detection and PHP is that the site is dynamically presented to mobile devices from the web server. Another advantage of using device detection and PHP is that it allows people the ability to opt-out of the mobile presentation and see the desktop presentation in their mobile browser. But this technique requires a server that is running PHP.

If this book is your entry to mobile web design, I hope it has been a clearly presented introduction to how you can learn and practice some useful techniques. If you have already done some mobile design, I hope one or more of these techniques have broadened your mobile experience.

Most importantly, I hope this book is just a first step to learning a lot more about responsive design that progressively enhances your web sites for the mobile context. Be sure to read some of the additional resources listed on the companion web site: http://www.mobilizingwebsites.net/

Good luck and happy mobilizing!

INDEX